Deacon Cartoons

Joe McKeever

Parson's Porch & Company

Parson's Porch Books

Deacon Cartoons
ISBN: Softcover 978-0692639344
Copyright © 2016 by Joe McKeever

All rights reserved. No part of this book may be reproduced or transmitted in any form or by any means, electronic or mechanical, including photocopying, recording, or by any information storage and retrieval system, without permission in writing from the publisher.

To order additional copies of this book, contact:

Parson's Porch Books

1-423-475-7308

www.parsonsporch.com

Parson's Porch Books is an imprint of Parson's Porch & Company (PP&C) in Cleveland, Tennessee. PP&C is an innovative company which raises money by publishing books of noted authors, representing all genres. All donations from contributors and profits from publishing are shared with the poor.

Deacon Cartoons

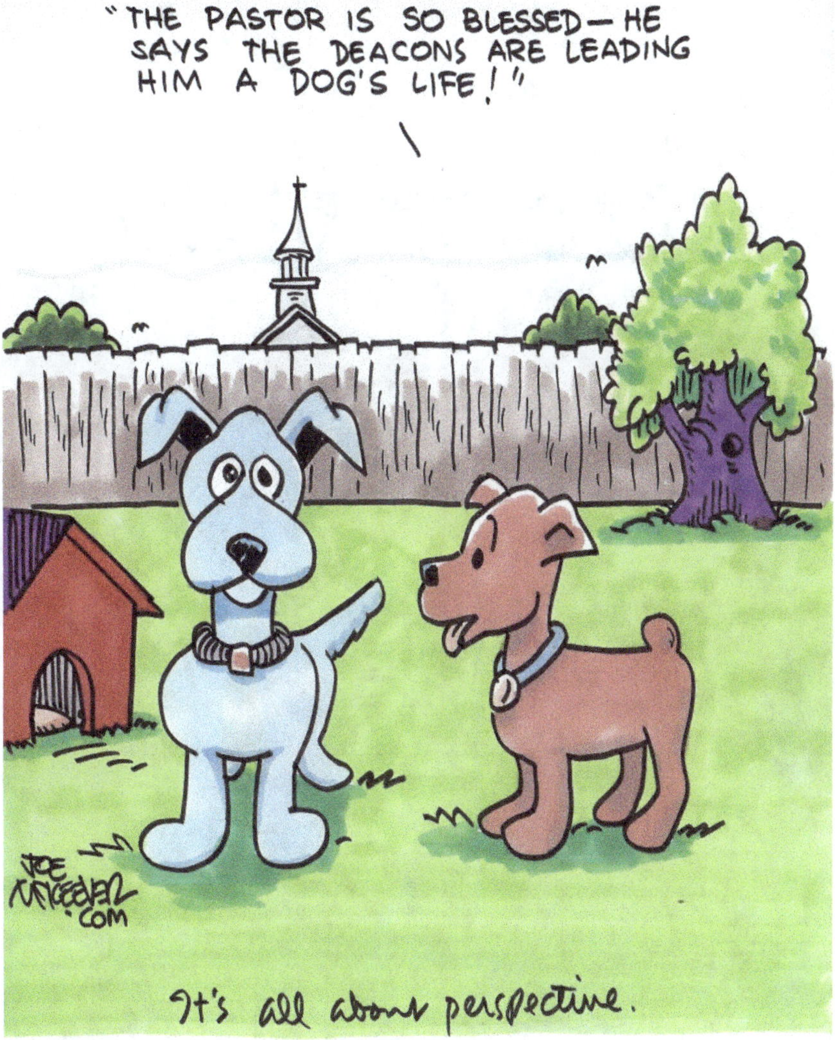
"THE PASTOR IS SO BLESSED— HE SAYS THE DEACONS ARE LEADING HIM A DOG'S LIFE!"
JOE McKEEVER .COM
It's all about perspective.

"WHAT FLOWER SAYS 'I'M SORRY YOUR HUSBAND DIDN'T MAKE DEACON, BUT I'M SURE HE WILL NEXT TIME'?"

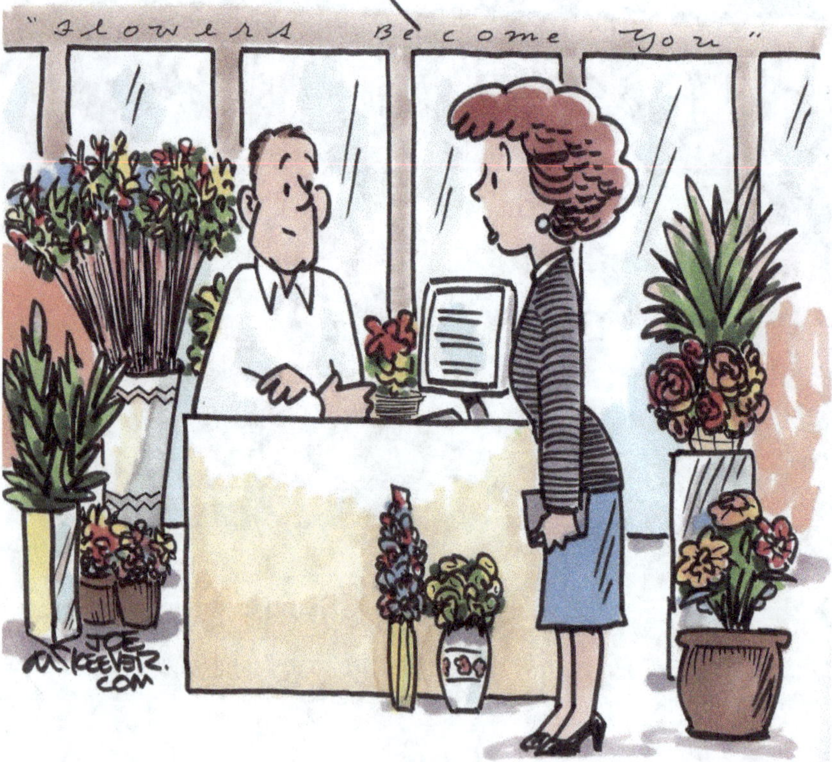
"Flowers Become You"
JOE McKEEVER.COM

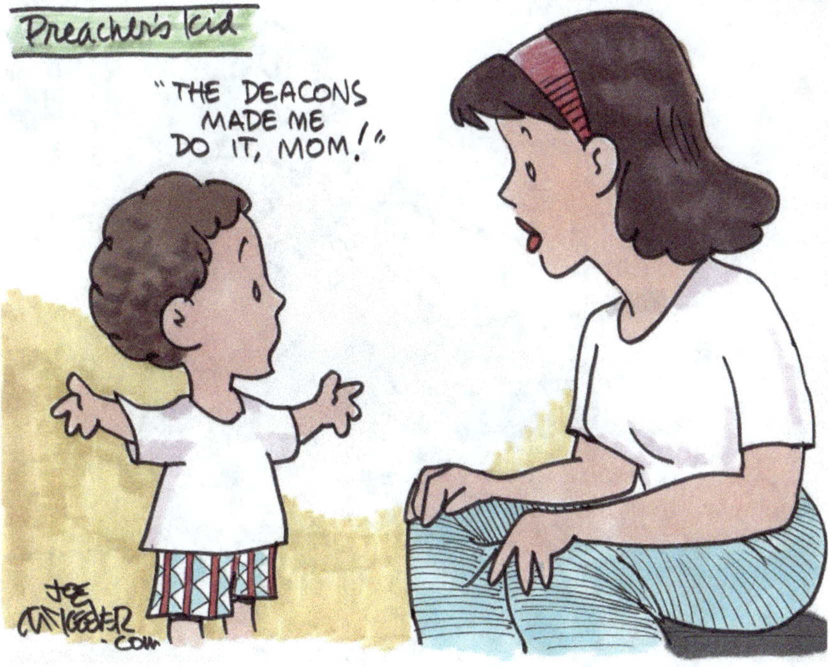
Preacher's Kid
"THE DEACONS MADE ME DO IT, MOM!"
JOE McKEEVER .COM

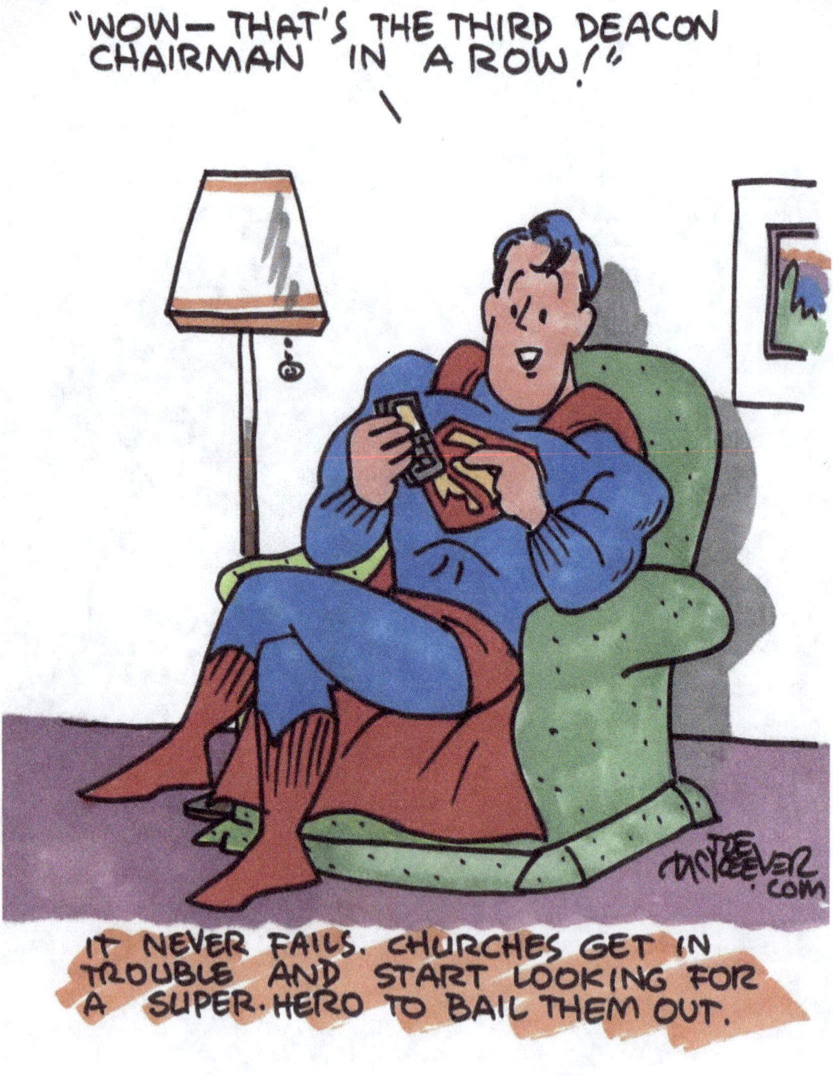
"WOW— THAT'S THE THIRD DEACON CHAIRMAN IN A ROW!"
JOE McKEEVER .com
IT NEVER FAILS. CHURCHES GET IN TROUBLE AND START LOOKING FOR A SUPER-HERO TO BAIL THEM OUT.

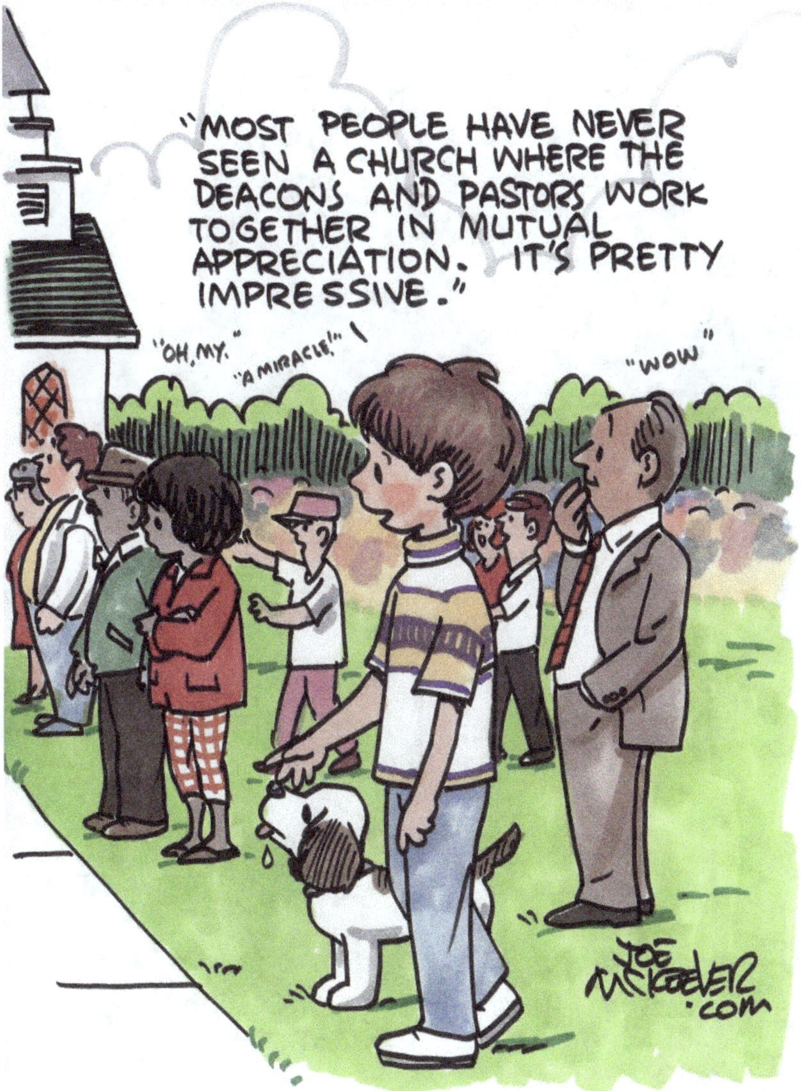
"MOST PEOPLE HAVE NEVER SEEN A CHURCH WHERE THE DEACONS AND PASTORS WORK TOGETHER IN MUTUAL APPRECIATION. IT'S PRETTY IMPRESSIVE."
"OH, MY."
"A MIRACLE!"
"WOW"
JOE MCKEEVER .com

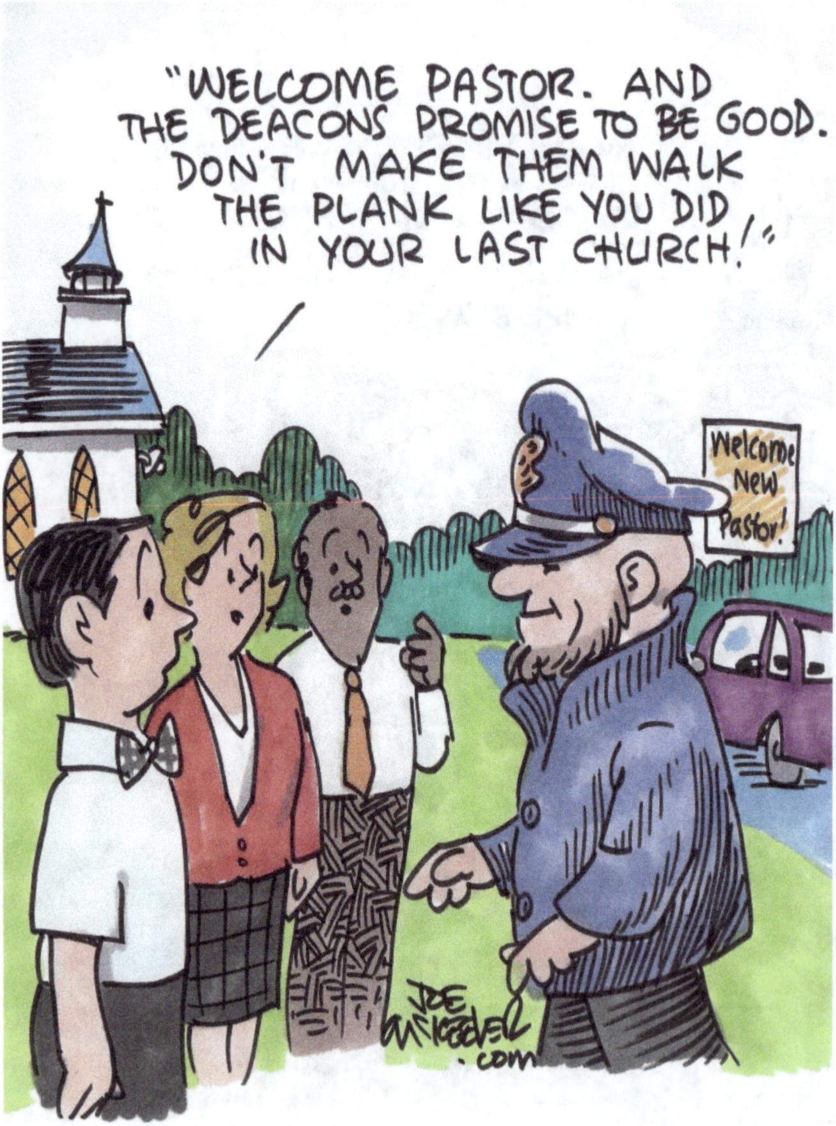
"WELCOME PASTOR. AND THE DEACONS PROMISE TO BE GOOD. DON'T MAKE THEM WALK THE PLANK LIKE YOU DID IN YOUR LAST CHURCH!"
Welcome New Pastor!
JOE McKEEVER .com

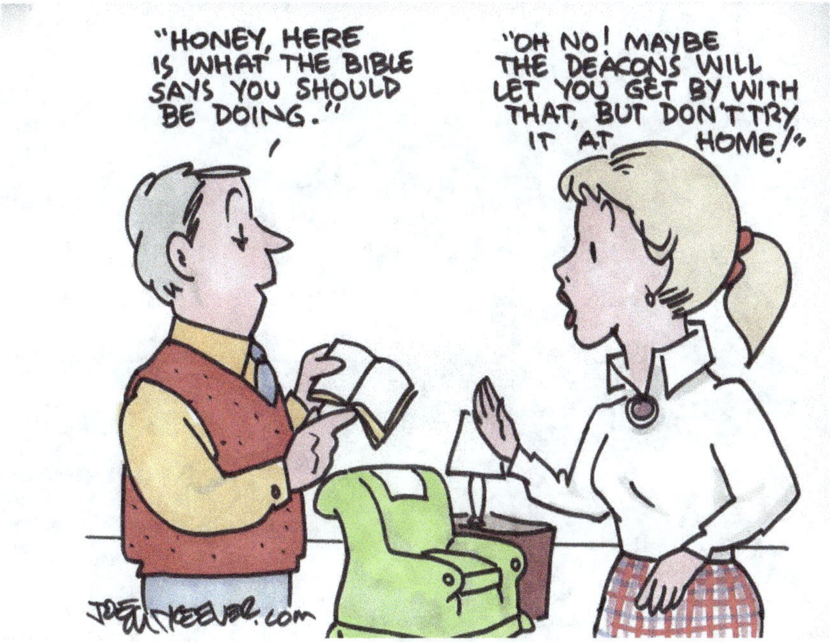
"HONEY, HERE IS WHAT THE BIBLE SAYS YOU SHOULD BE DOING."
"OH NO! MAYBE THE DEACONS WILL LET YOU GET BY WITH THAT, BUT DON'T TRY IT AT HOME!"
JOEMCKEEVER.com

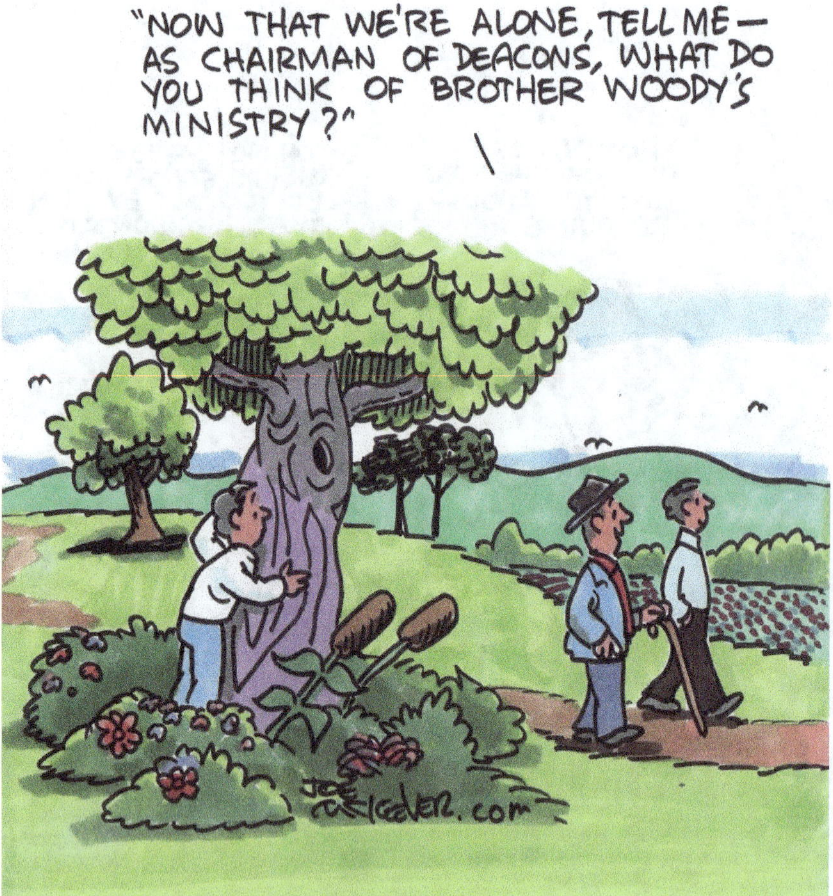
"NOW THAT WE'RE ALONE, TELL ME—AS CHAIRMAN OF DEACONS, WHAT DO YOU THINK OF BROTHER WOODY'S MINISTRY?"

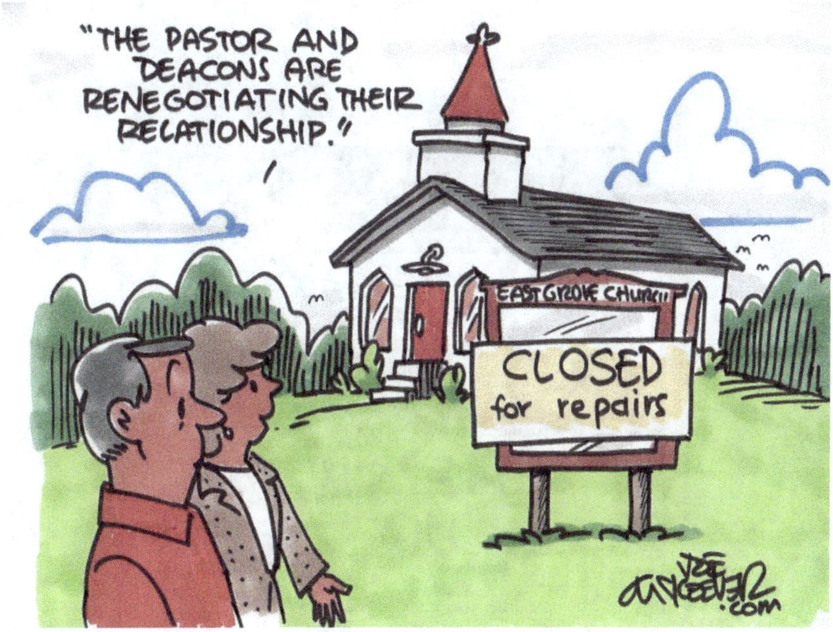
"THE PASTOR AND DEACONS ARE RENEGOTIATING THEIR RELATIONSHIP."
EAST GROVE CHURCH
CLOSED for repairs
JOE McKEEVER.com

We have to take good care of our leadership.

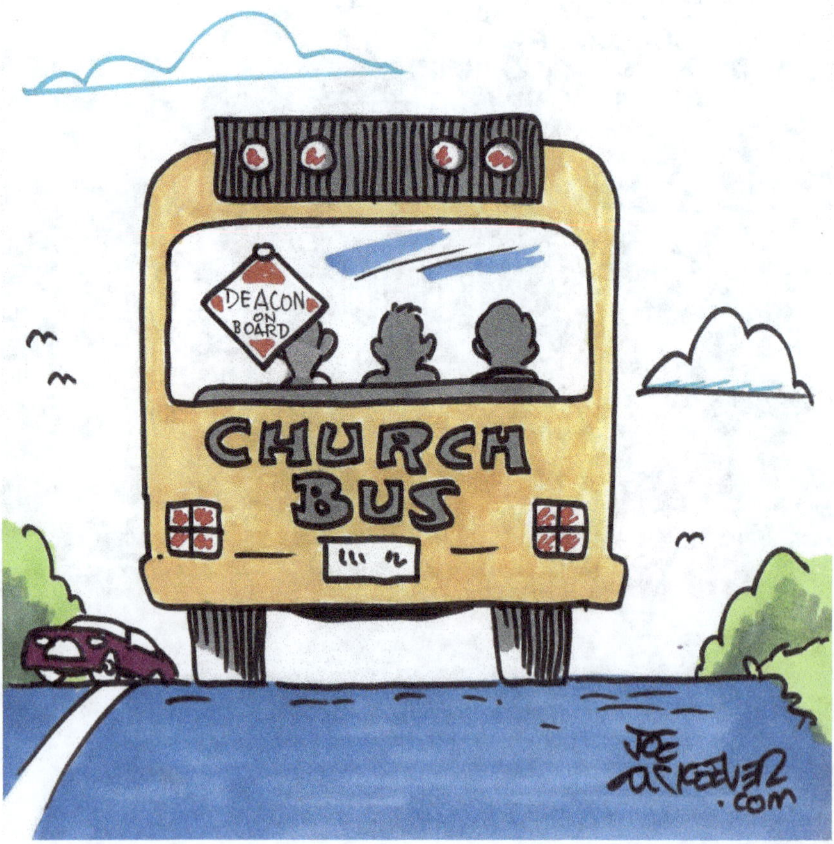
DEACON ON BOARD
CHURCH BUS
JOE McKEEVER .com

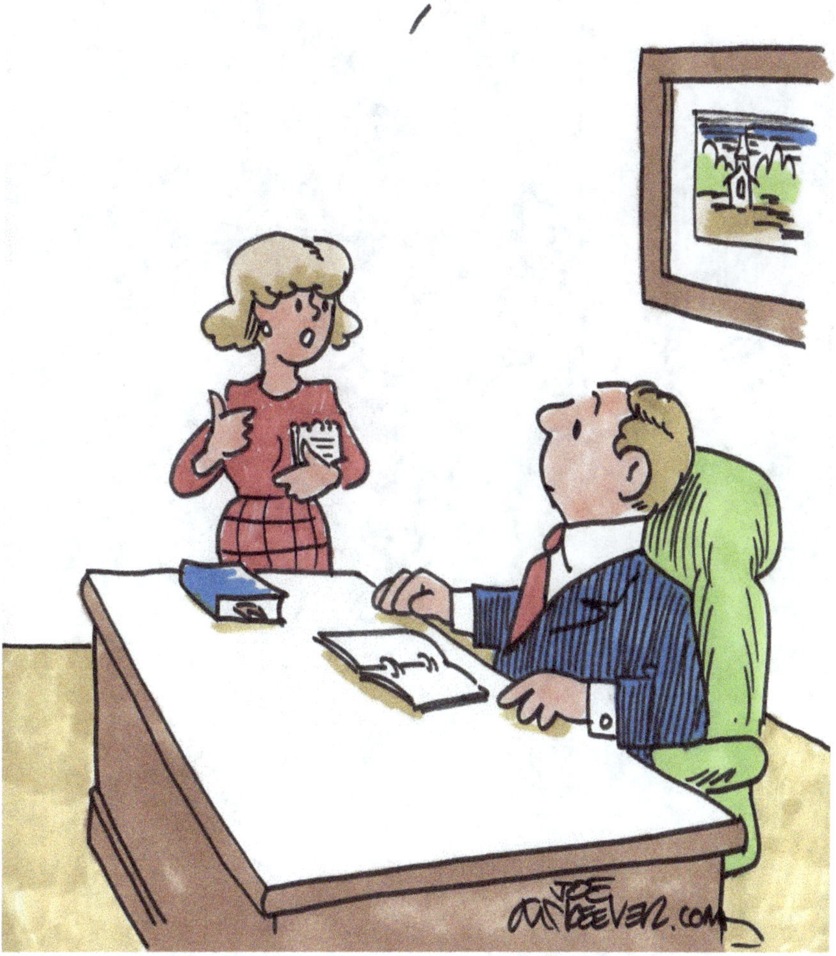
JOE McKEEVER.COM

"DEACON JACKSON SAYS HE WANTS TO SEE 'THE HOSS.' BE CAREFUL, PASTOR— HE'S WEARING SPURS."

"SORRY GUYS. WE NEED TO BE CAREFUL.
THE DEACONS' CATS ARE WATCHING US."

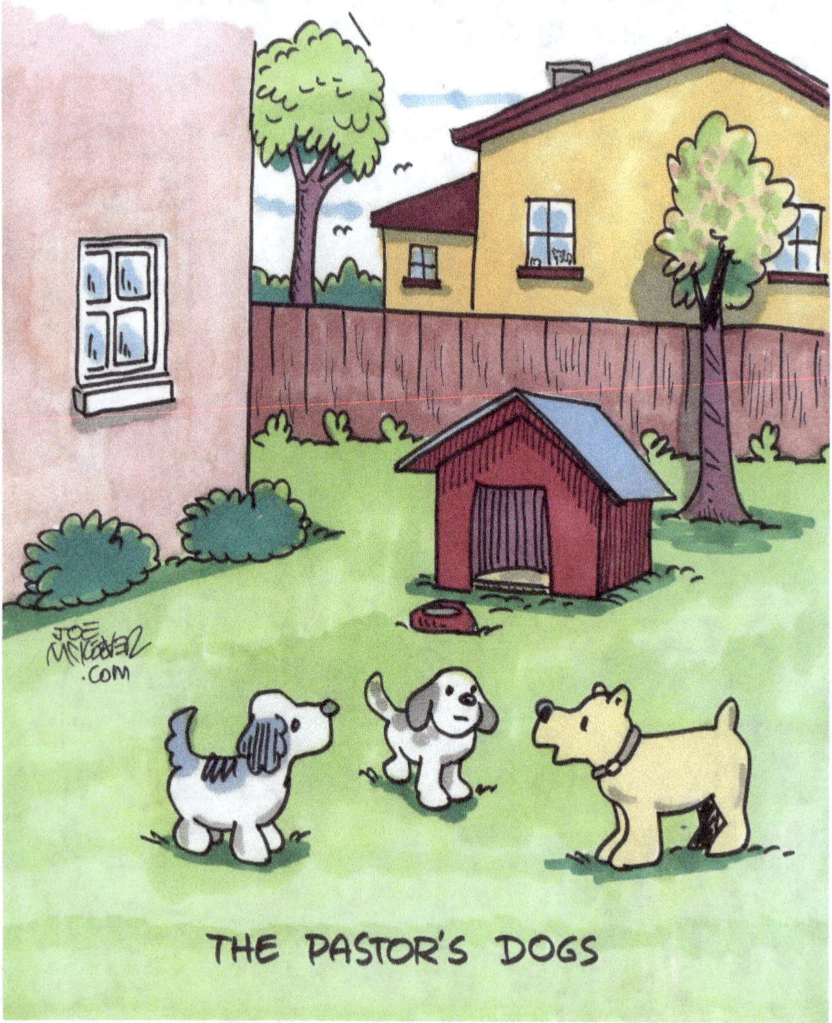
THE PASTOR'S DOGS

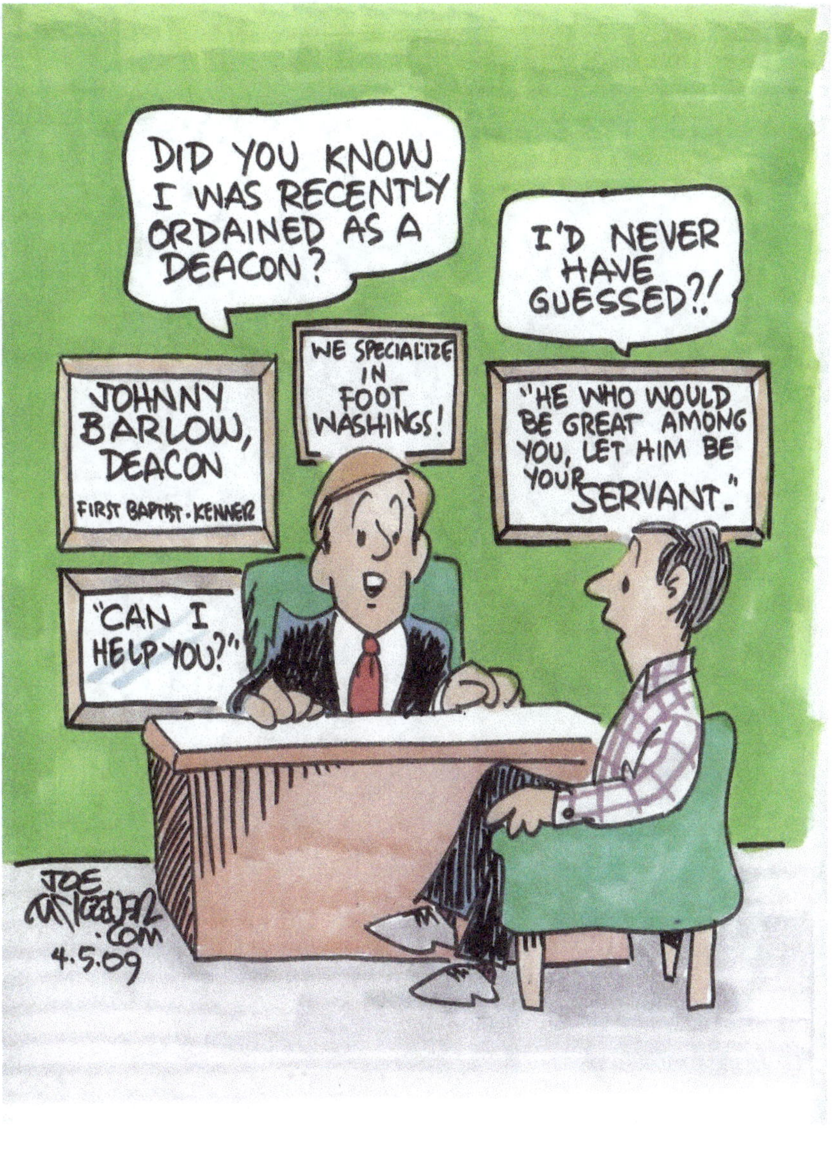
DID YOU KNOW I WAS RECENTLY ORDAINED AS A DEACON?
I'D NEVER HAVE GUESSED?!
JOHNNY BARLOW, DEACON
FIRST BAPTIST · KENNER
WE SPECIALIZE IN FOOT WASHINGS!
"HE WHO WOULD BE GREAT AMONG YOU, LET HIM BE YOUR SERVANT."
"CAN I HELP YOU?"
JOE MCKEEVER.COM
4.5.09

"I THOUGHT HE MIGHT BE DEACON MATERIAL FOR OUR CHURCH— BUT THAT MUCH JOY WORRIES ME!"

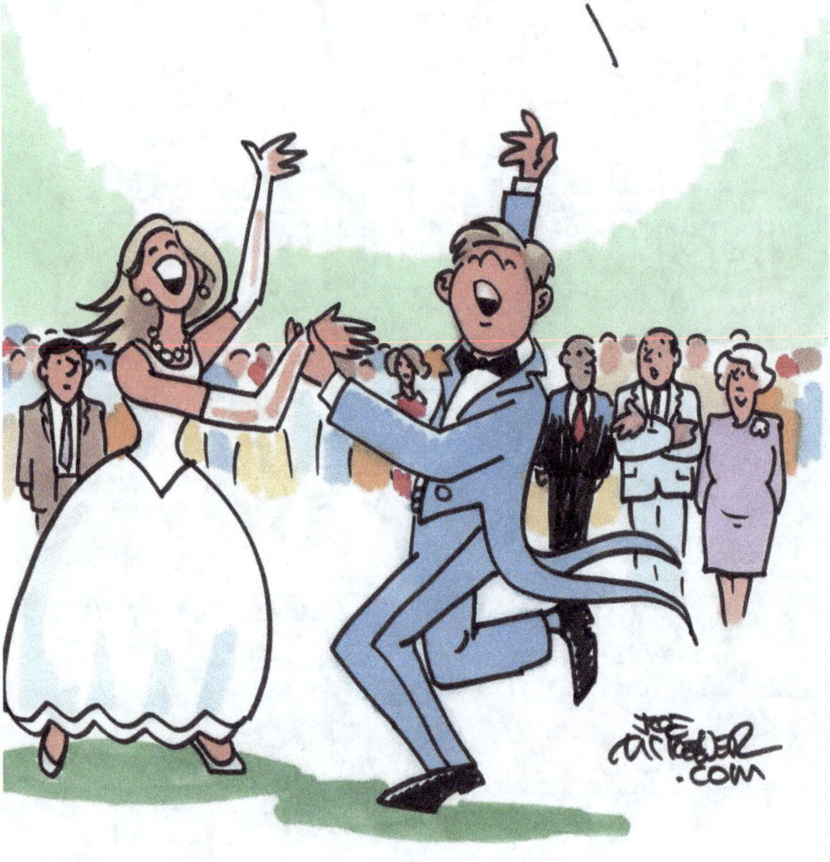

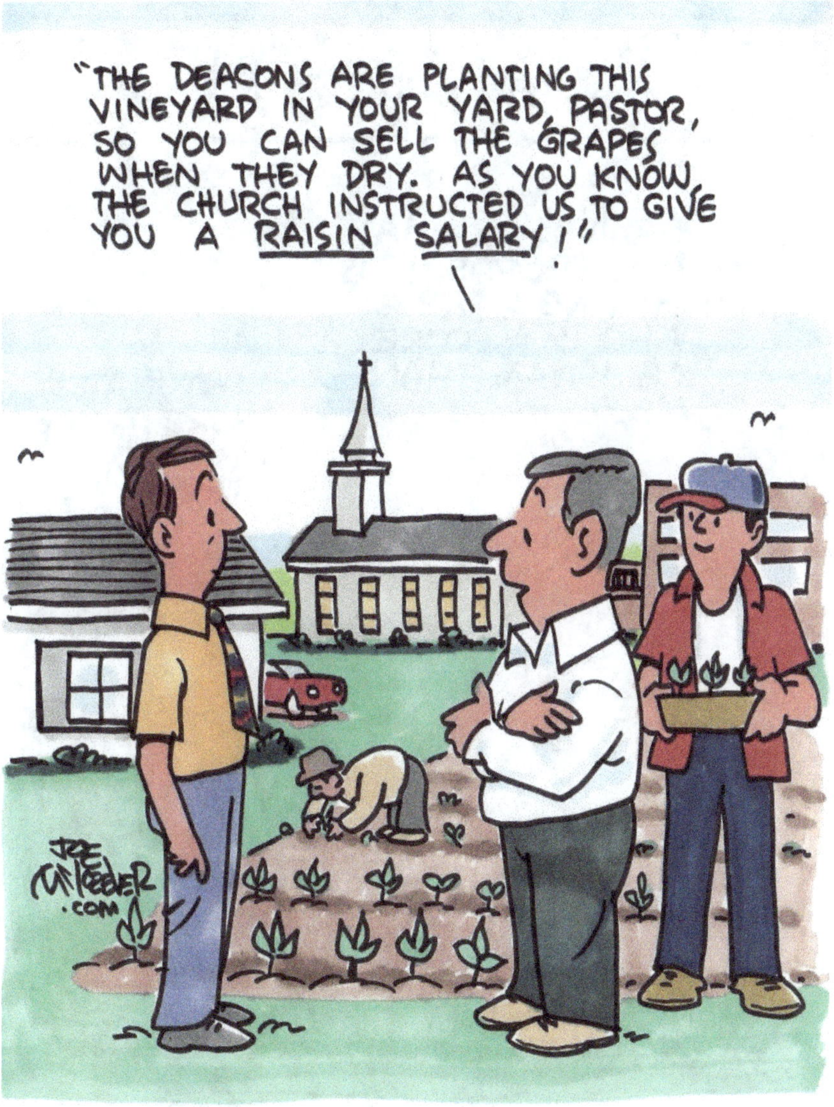
"THE DEACONS ARE PLANTING THIS VINEYARD IN YOUR YARD, PASTOR, SO YOU CAN SELL THE GRAPES WHEN THEY DRY. AS YOU KNOW, THE CHURCH INSTRUCTED US TO GIVE YOU A RAISIN SALARY!"
JOE MCKEEVER .COM

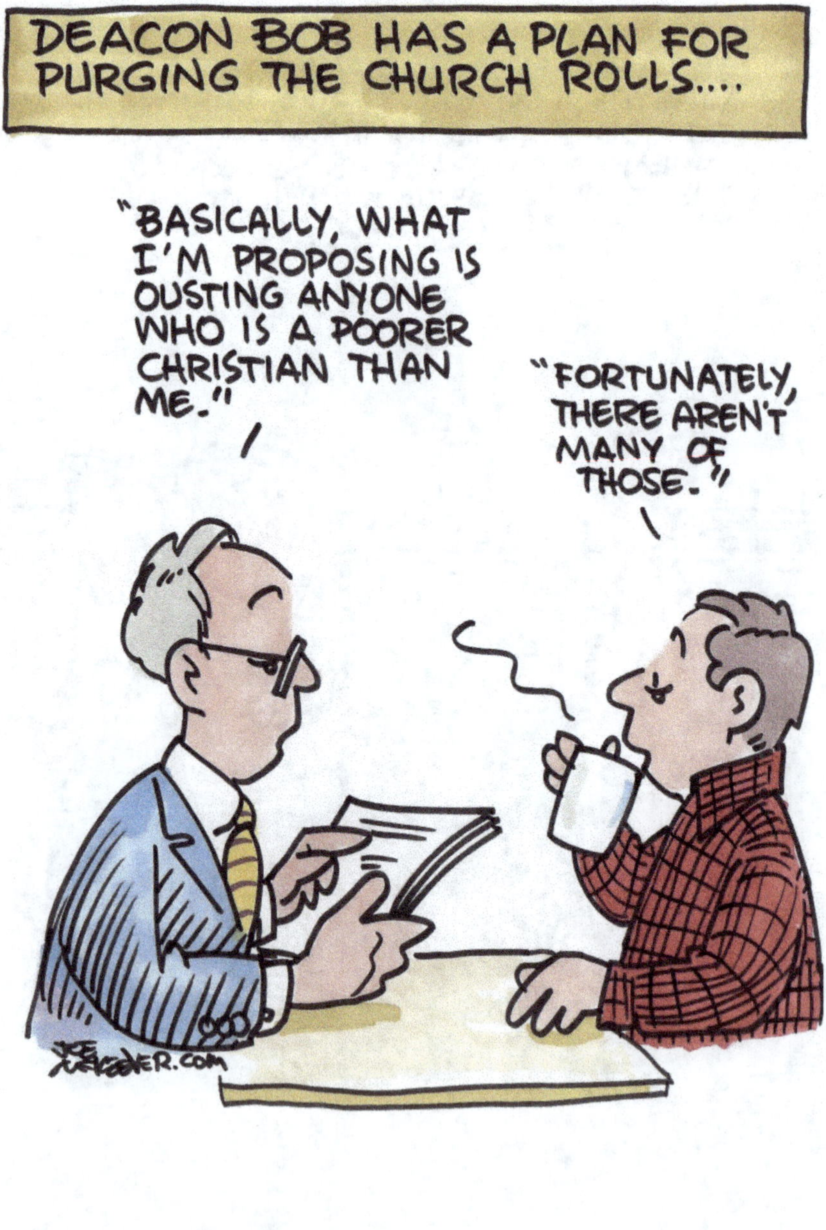
DEACON BOB HAS A PLAN FOR PURGING THE CHURCH ROLLS....
"BASICALLY, WHAT I'M PROPOSING IS OUSTING ANYONE WHO IS A POORER CHRISTIAN THAN ME."
"FORTUNATELY, THERE AREN'T MANY OF THOSE."
JOE McKEEVER.COM

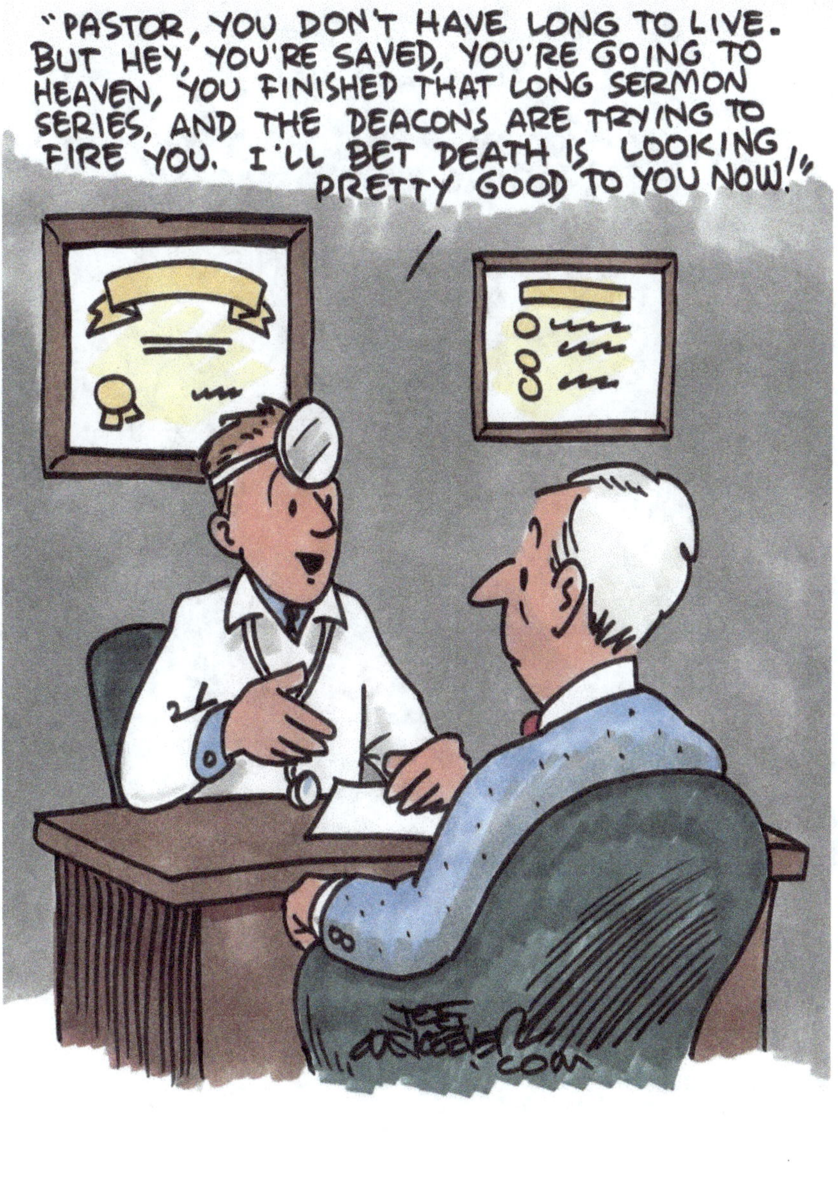
"PASTOR, YOU DON'T HAVE LONG TO LIVE. BUT HEY, YOU'RE SAVED, YOU'RE GOING TO HEAVEN, YOU FINISHED THAT LONG SERMON SERIES, AND THE DEACONS ARE TRYING TO FIRE YOU. I'LL BET DEATH IS LOOKING PRETTY GOOD TO YOU NOW!"

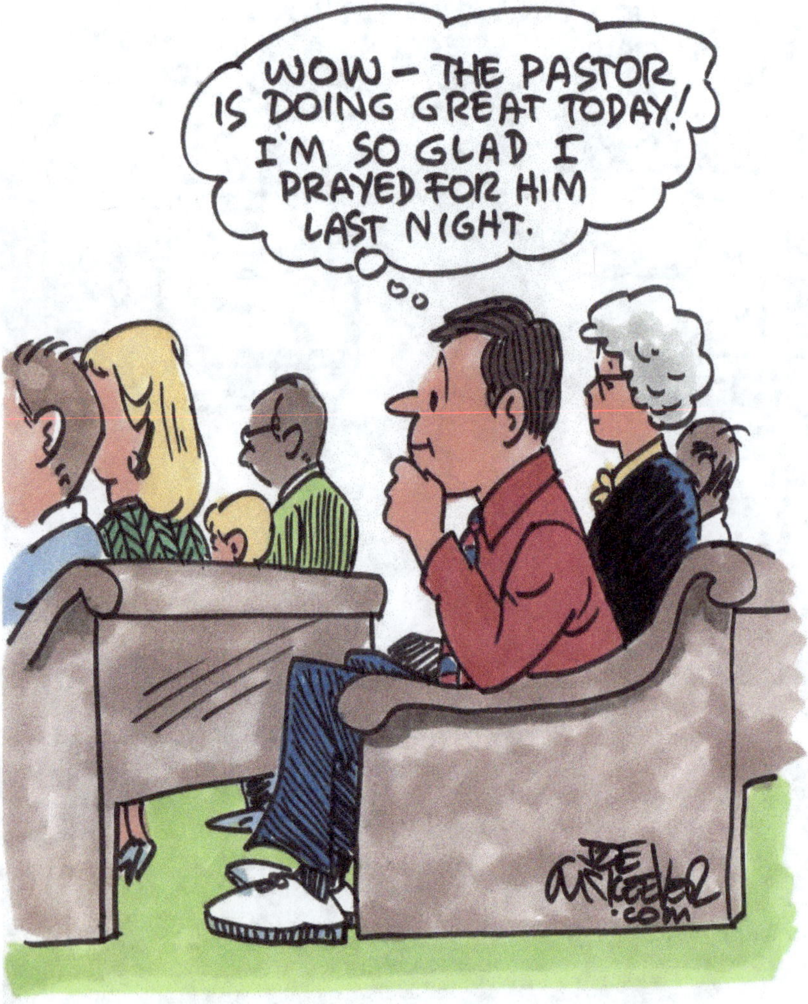
WOW - THE PASTOR IS DOING GREAT TODAY! I'M SO GLAD I PRAYED FOR HIM LAST NIGHT.
JOE McKEEVER .com

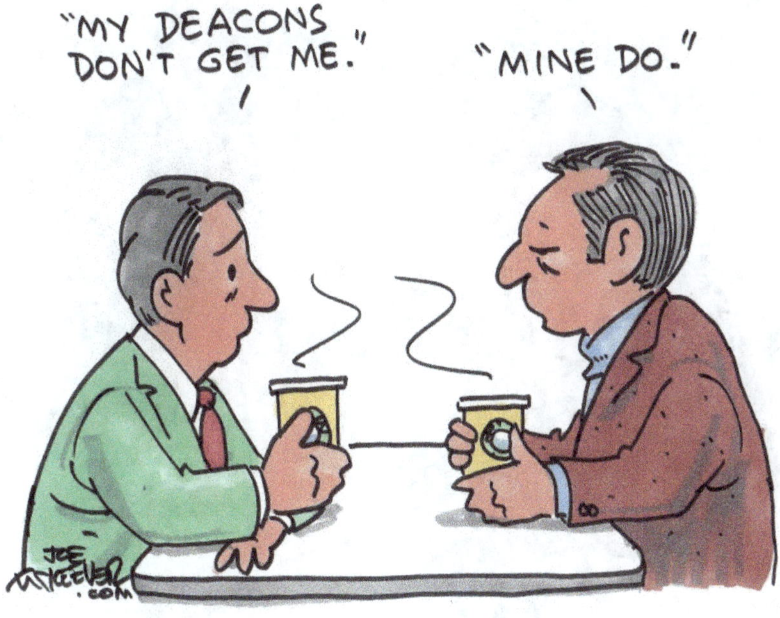
"MY DEACONS DON'T GET ME."
"MINE DO."
JOE McKEEVER .com

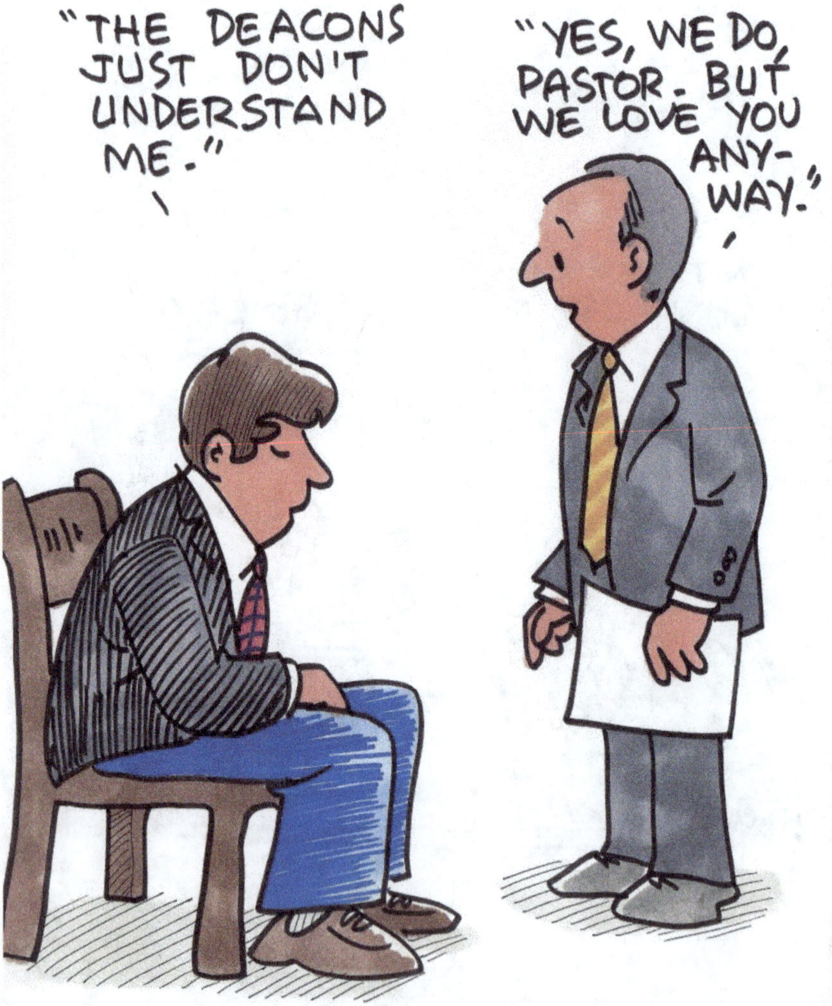
"THE DEACONS JUST DON'T UNDERSTAND ME."
"YES, WE DO, PASTOR. BUT WE LOVE YOU ANYWAY."

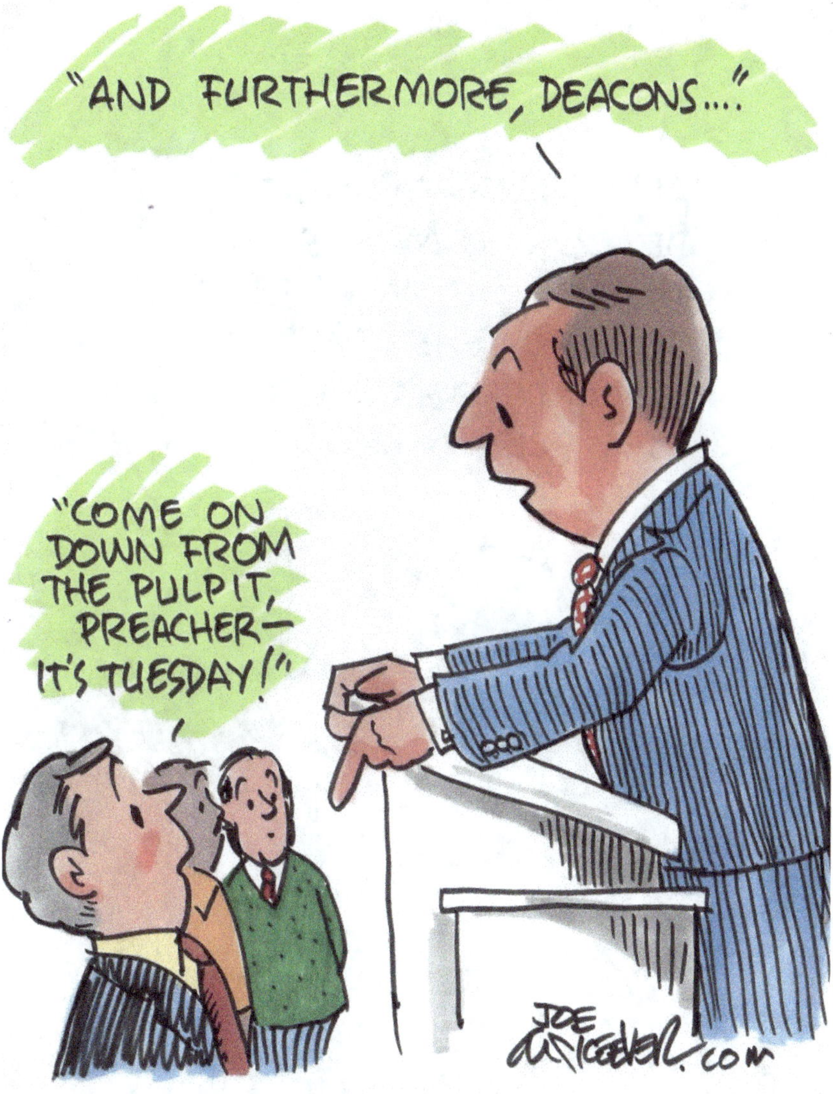
"AND FURTHERMORE, DEACONS..."
"COME ON DOWN FROM THE PULPIT, PREACHER— IT'S TUESDAY!"
JOE McKEEVER.com

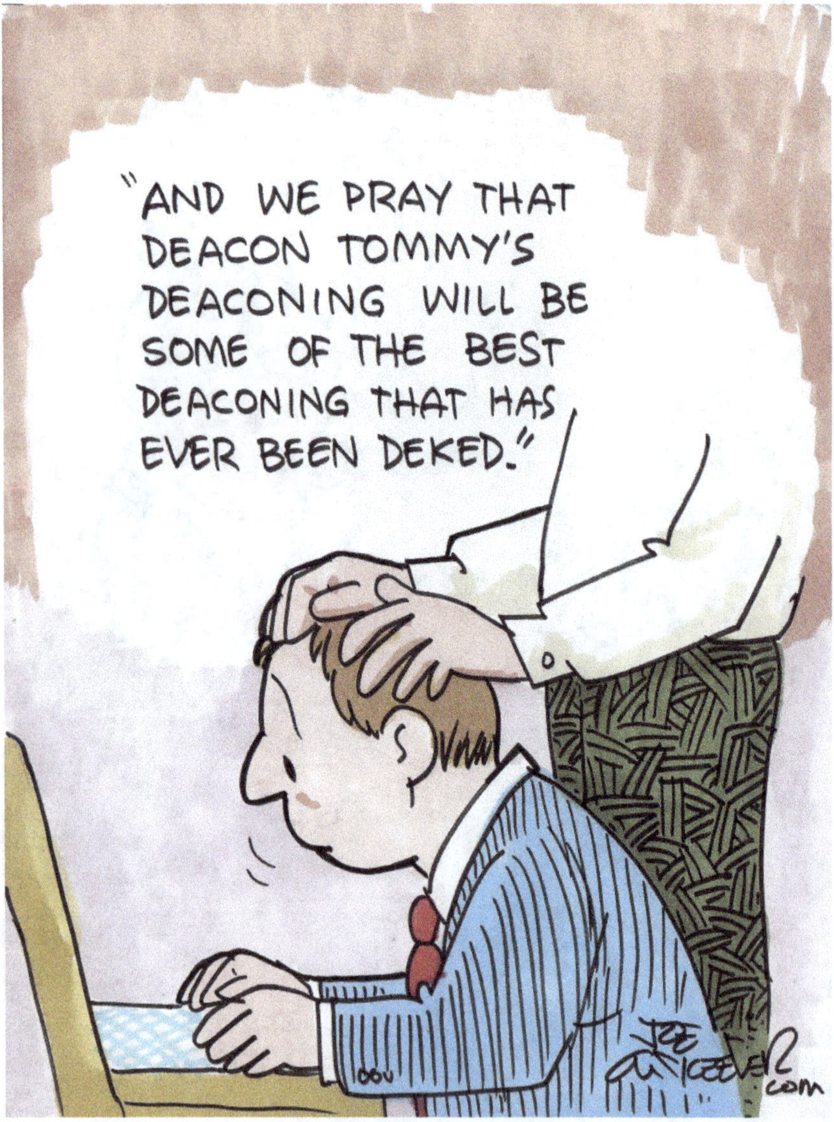
"AND WE PRAY THAT DEACON TOMMY'S DEACONING WILL BE SOME OF THE BEST DEACONING THAT HAS EVER BEEN DEKED."
JOE MCKEEVER.com

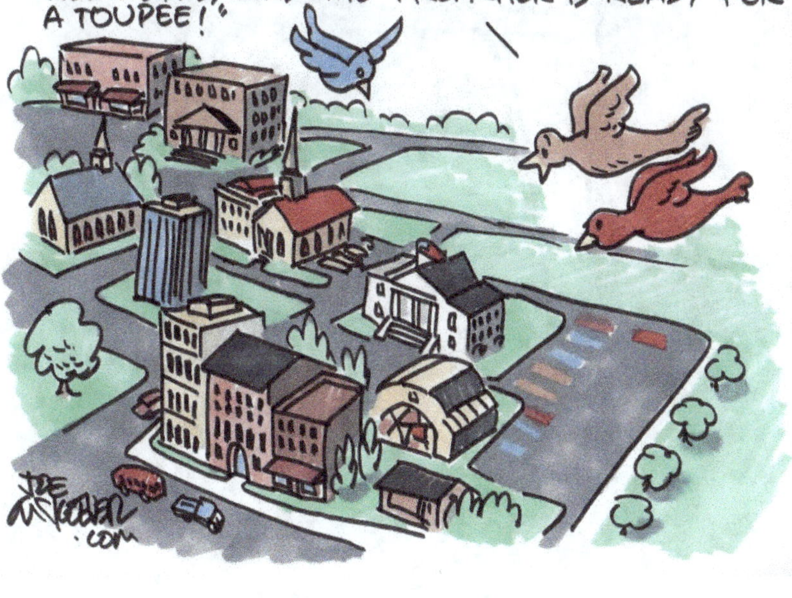
JOE McKEEVER
.COM

"THE CHURCH NEEDS A NEW ROOF, THE DEACON NEEDS TO TURN OFF THE T.V. AND MEET HIS NEIGHBORS, AND THE PREACHER IS READY FOR A TOUPEE!"

IN CHILDREN'S GAMES AS IN LIFE, IT'S ALL EASIER IF YOU HAVE A FRIEND TO GIVE YOU A SHOVE.

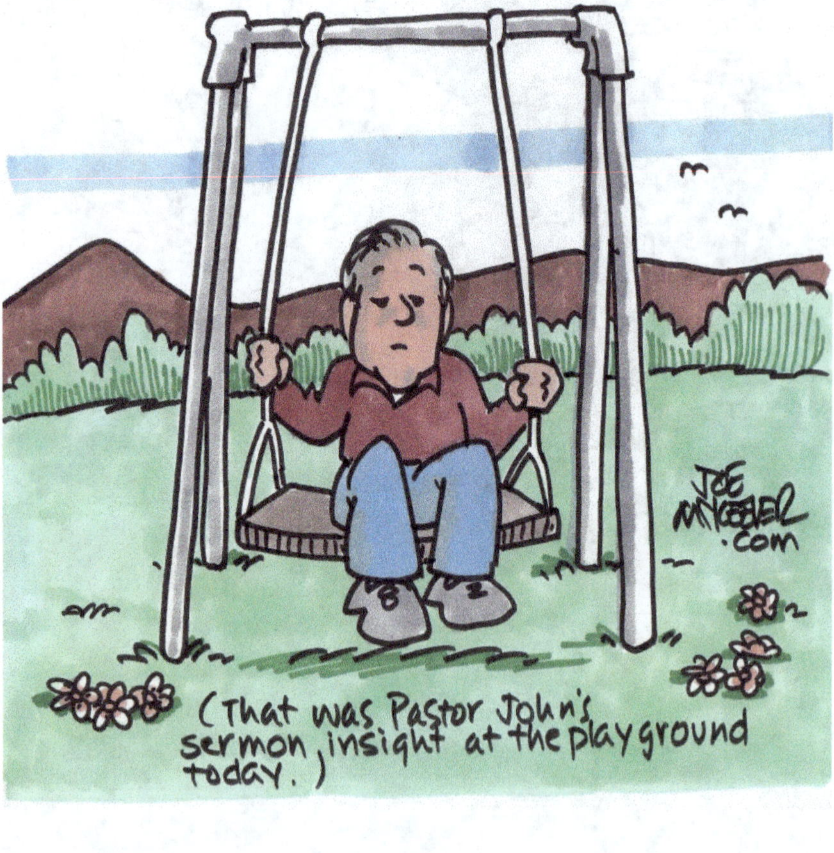
JOE MCKEEVER .com
(That was Pastor John's sermon insight at the playground today.)

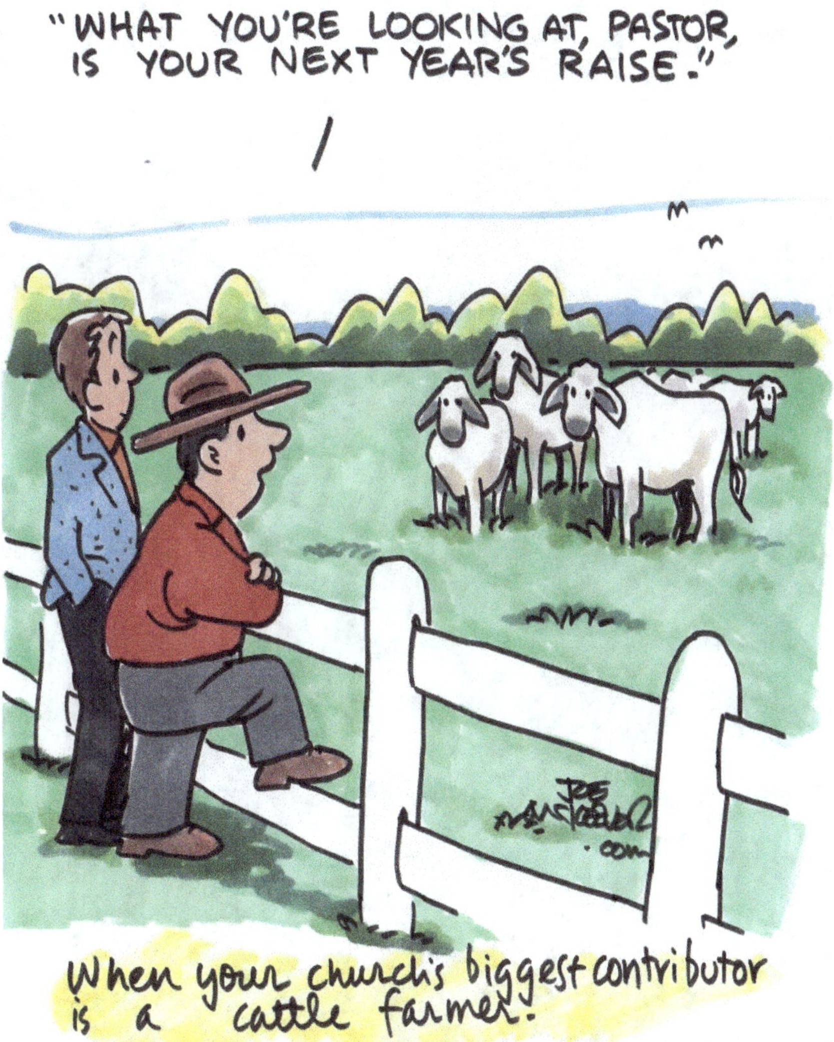
"WHAT YOU'RE LOOKING AT, PASTOR, IS YOUR NEXT YEAR'S RAISE."

When your church's biggest contributor is a cattle farmer!

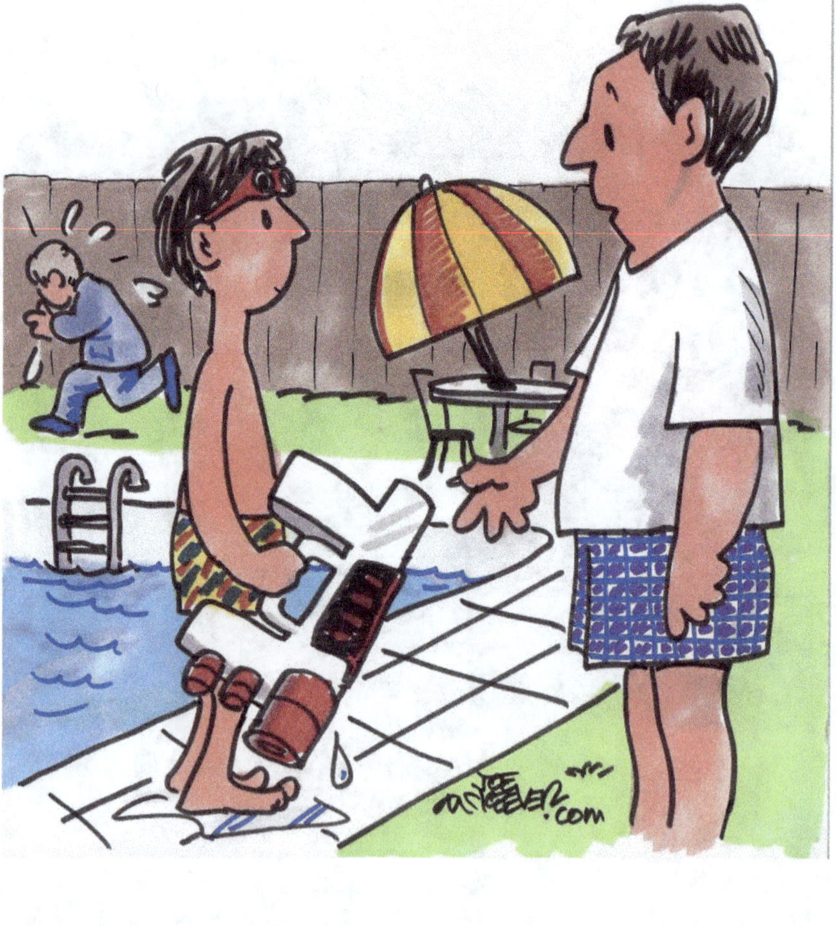

"SON, THAT WASN'T VERY NICE— BLASTING THE PASTOR AS PAYBACK FOR BAPTIZING YOU."

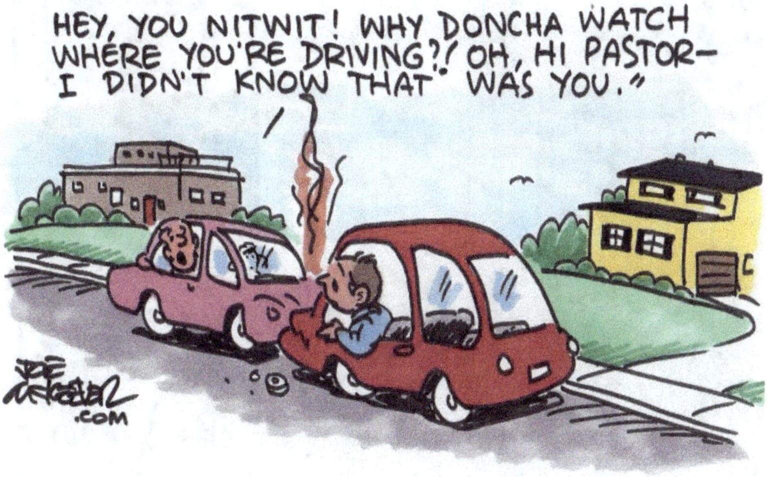
HEY, YOU NITWIT! WHY DONCHA WATCH WHERE YOU'RE DRIVING?! OH, HI PASTOR– I DIDN'T KNOW THAT WAS YOU."

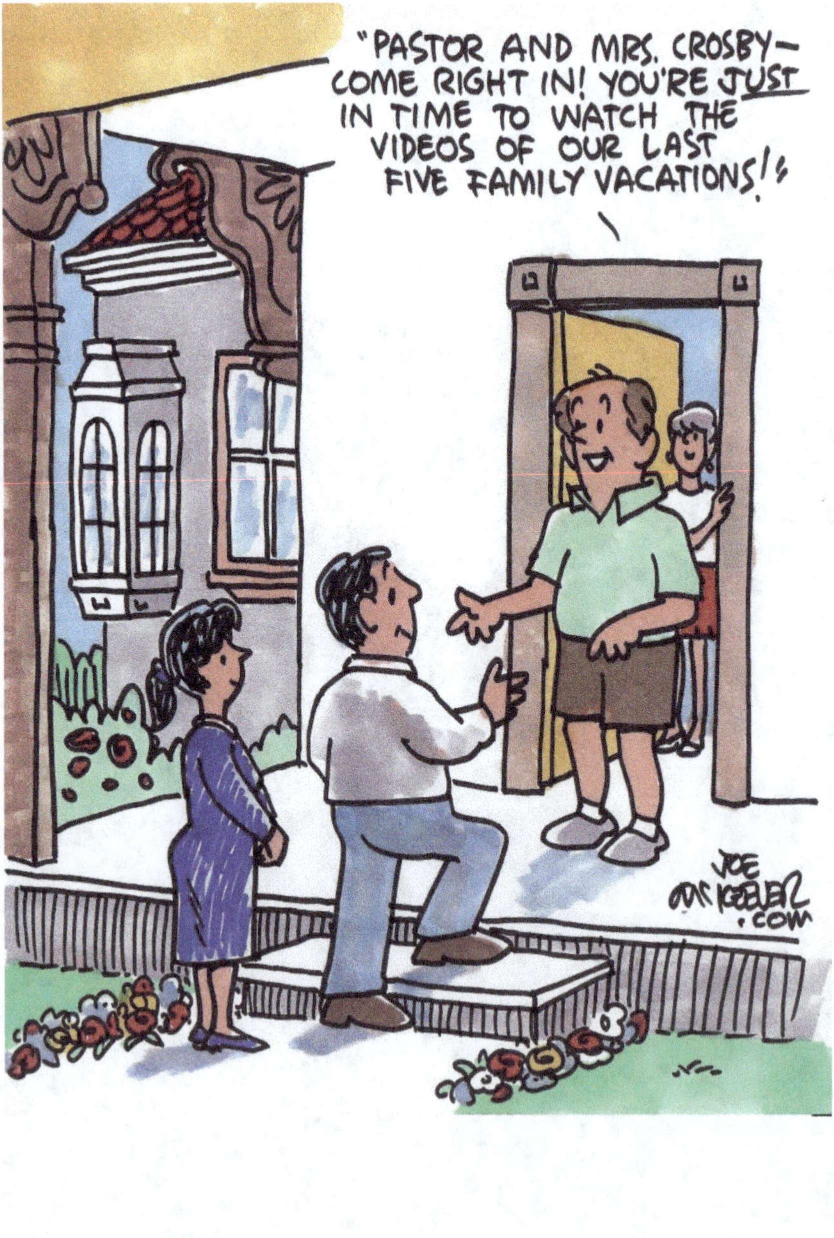
"PASTOR AND MRS. CROSBY—COME RIGHT IN! YOU'RE JUST IN TIME TO WATCH THE VIDEOS OF OUR LAST FIVE FAMILY VACATIONS!"
JOE MCKEEVER .COM

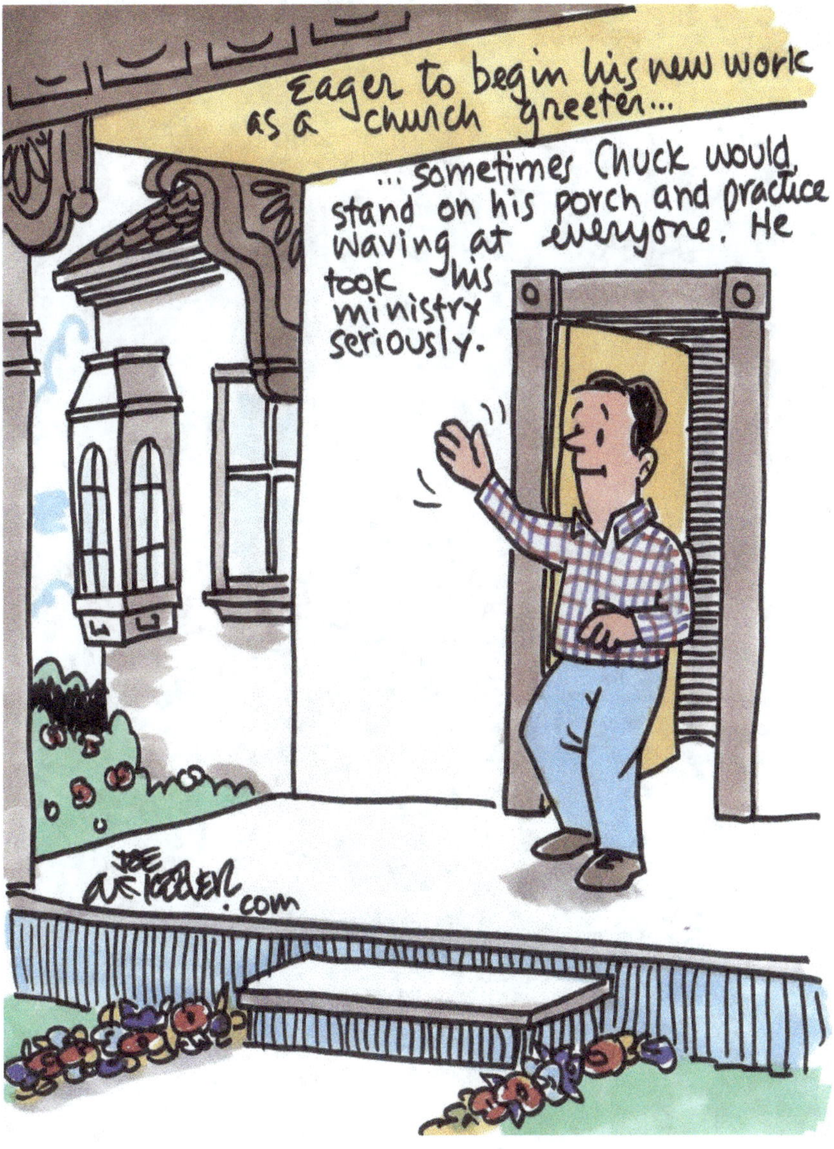
Eager to begin his new work as a church greeter...
...sometimes Chuck would stand on his porch and practice waving at everyone. He took his ministry seriously.
JOE McKEEVER.com

"CHARLIE IS MAKING A MOTION THAT CHRISTMAS BE ALLOWED TO HAPPEN ON DECEMBER 25TH THIS YEAR."

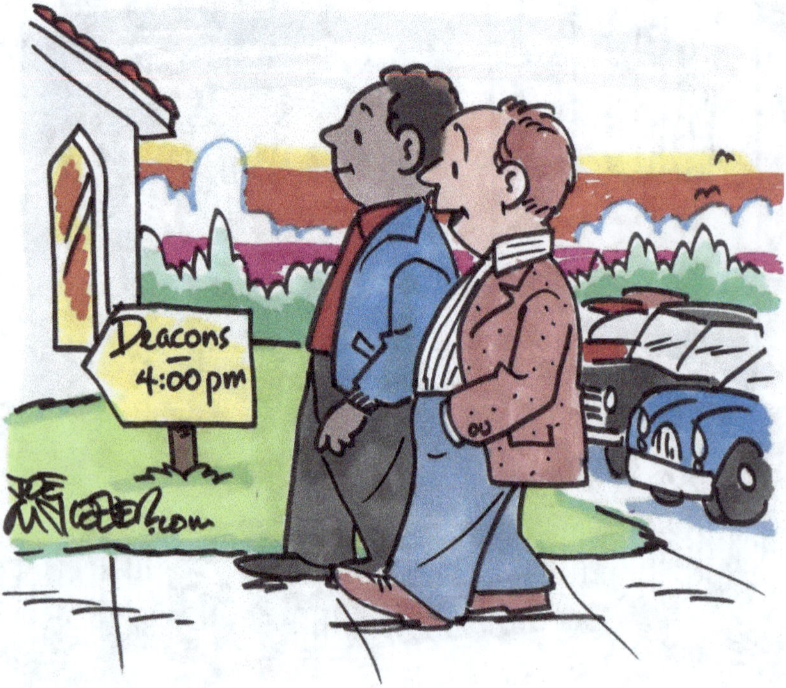
Deacons
—
4:00 pm

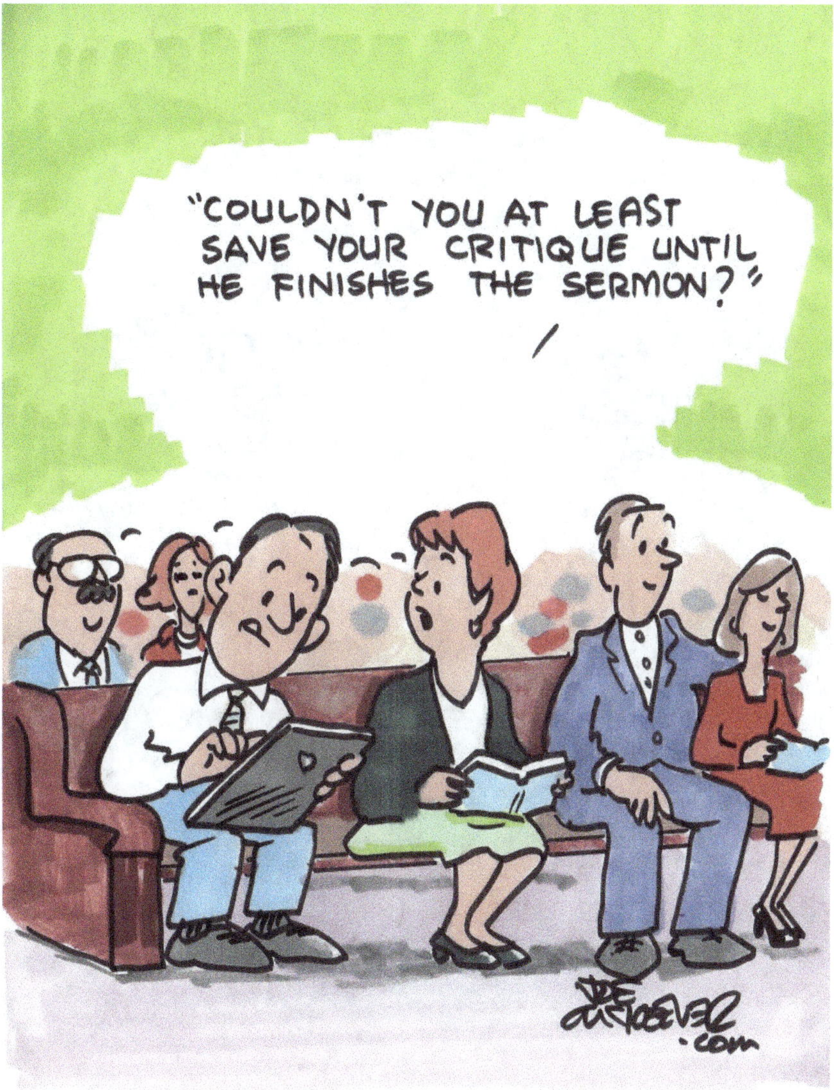
"COULDN'T YOU AT LEAST SAVE YOUR CRITIQUE UNTIL HE FINISHES THE SERMON?"
.com

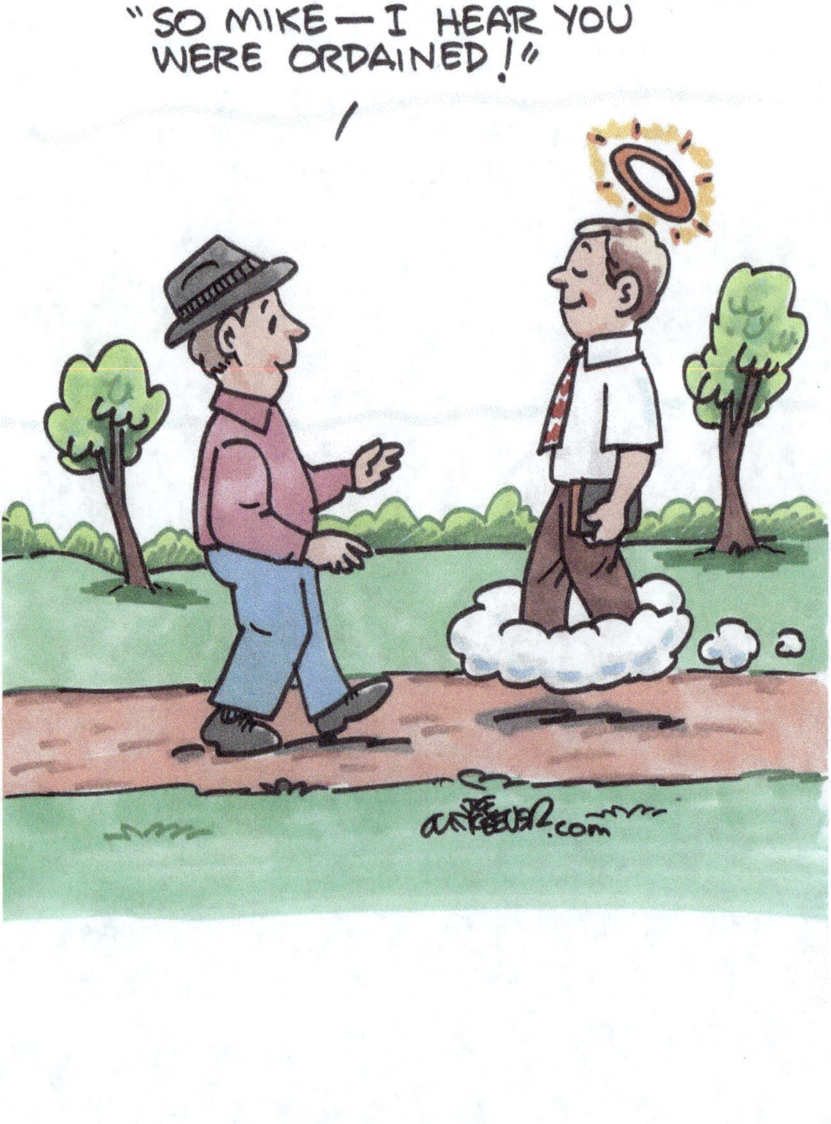
"SO MIKE — I HEAR YOU WERE ORDAINED!"

"AND LORD, WE THANK YOU THAT THERE IS A FRIEND WHO STICKS CLOSER THAN A BROTHER."

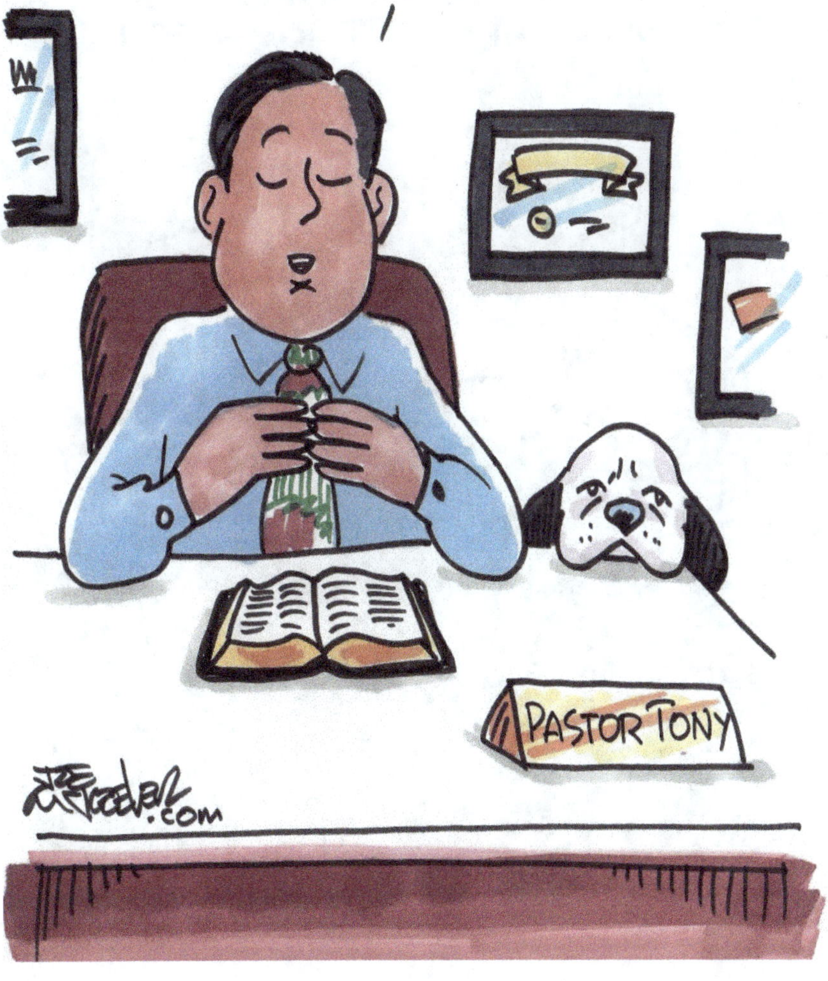
PASTOR TONY

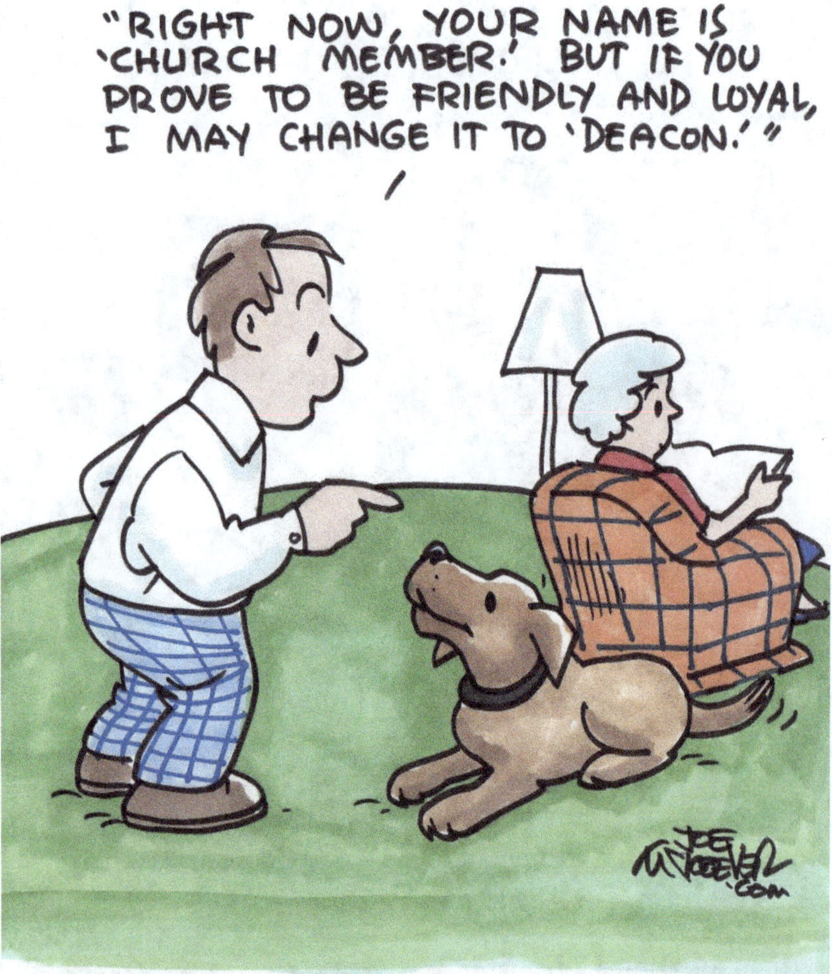
"RIGHT NOW, YOUR NAME IS 'CHURCH MEMBER.' BUT IF YOU PROVE TO BE FRIENDLY AND LOYAL, I MAY CHANGE IT TO 'DEACON.'"
JOE McKEEVER.com

HE'S BEEN WITH US A LONG TIME, HASN'T HE?
YES, THE DEACONS ARE CHECKING ON THE STATUTE OF LIMITATIONS FOR SOME OF HIS SERMONS!
CELEBRATING OUR PASTOR'S 25TH ANNIVERSARY!
JOE McKEEVER .COM

THE CHURCH STAFF LOVED THEIR LITTLE PRACTICAL JOKES. BUT THAT DAY, THE TRICK WITH PASTOR JACK BACKFIRED WHEN IT TURNED OUT THAT THE SCARY FIGURES IN THE JACK-IN-THE-BOX....

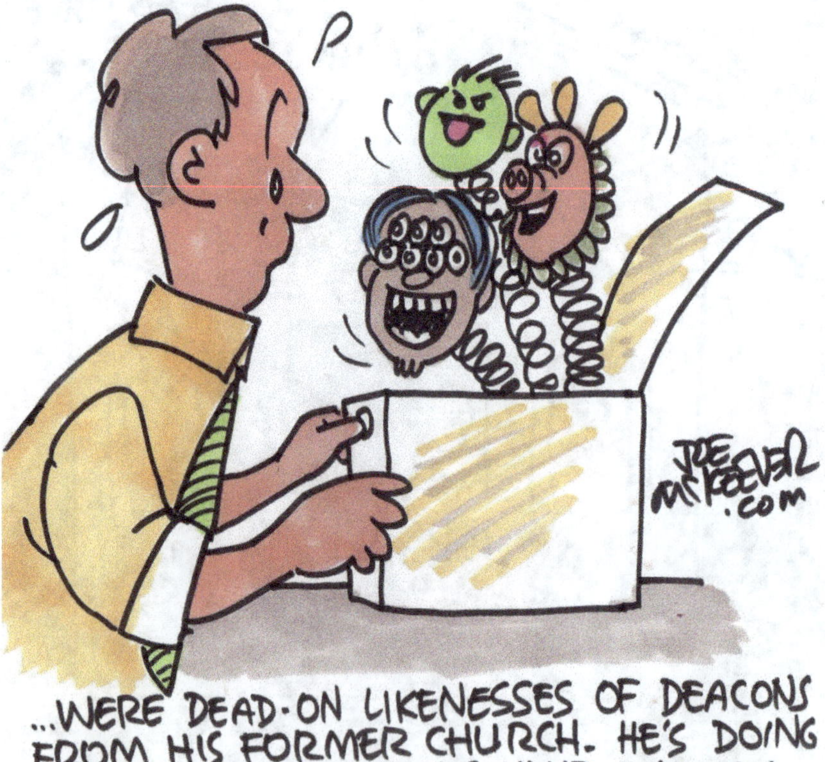
JOE McKEEVER
.com

...WERE DEAD-ON LIKENESSES OF DEACONS FROM HIS FORMER CHURCH. HE'S DOING NICELY IN THE CARDIAC UNIT, THOUGH.

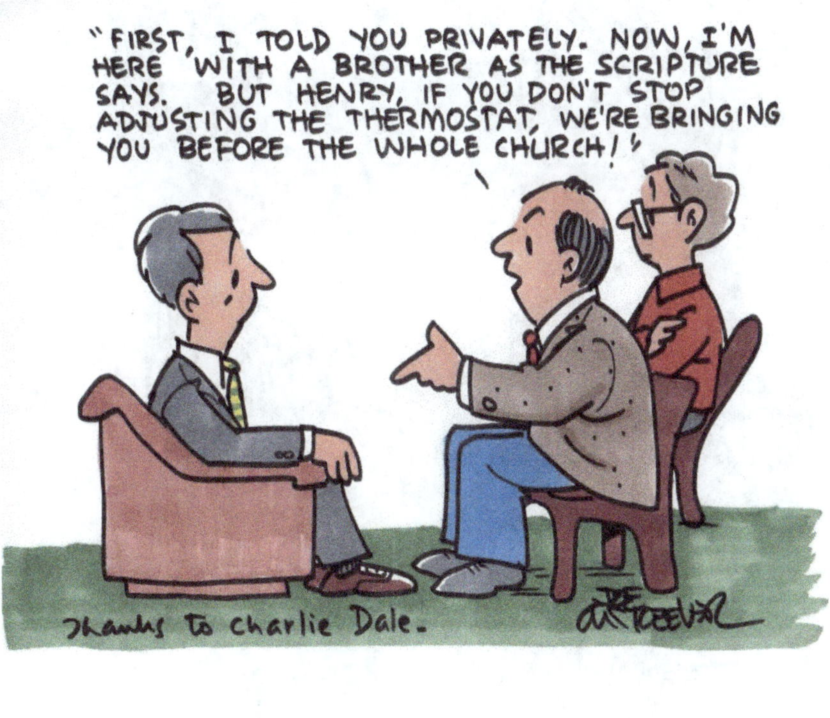
"FIRST, I TOLD YOU PRIVATELY. NOW, I'M HERE WITH A BROTHER AS THE SCRIPTURE SAYS. BUT HENRY, IF YOU DON'T STOP ADJUSTING THE THERMOSTAT, WE'RE BRINGING YOU BEFORE THE WHOLE CHURCH!"
Thanks to Charlie Dale.

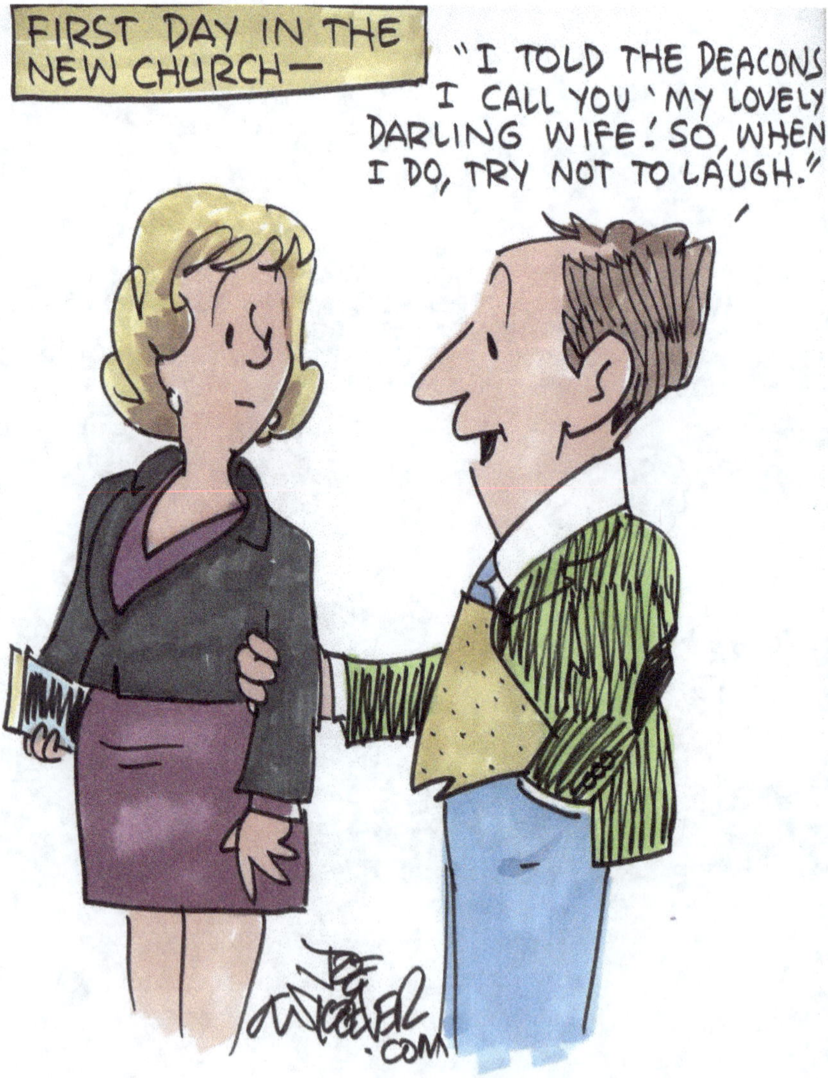
FIRST DAY IN THE NEW CHURCH—
"I TOLD THE DEACONS I CALL YOU 'MY LOVELY DARLING WIFE.' SO, WHEN I DO, TRY NOT TO LAUGH."
JOE McKEEVER .COM

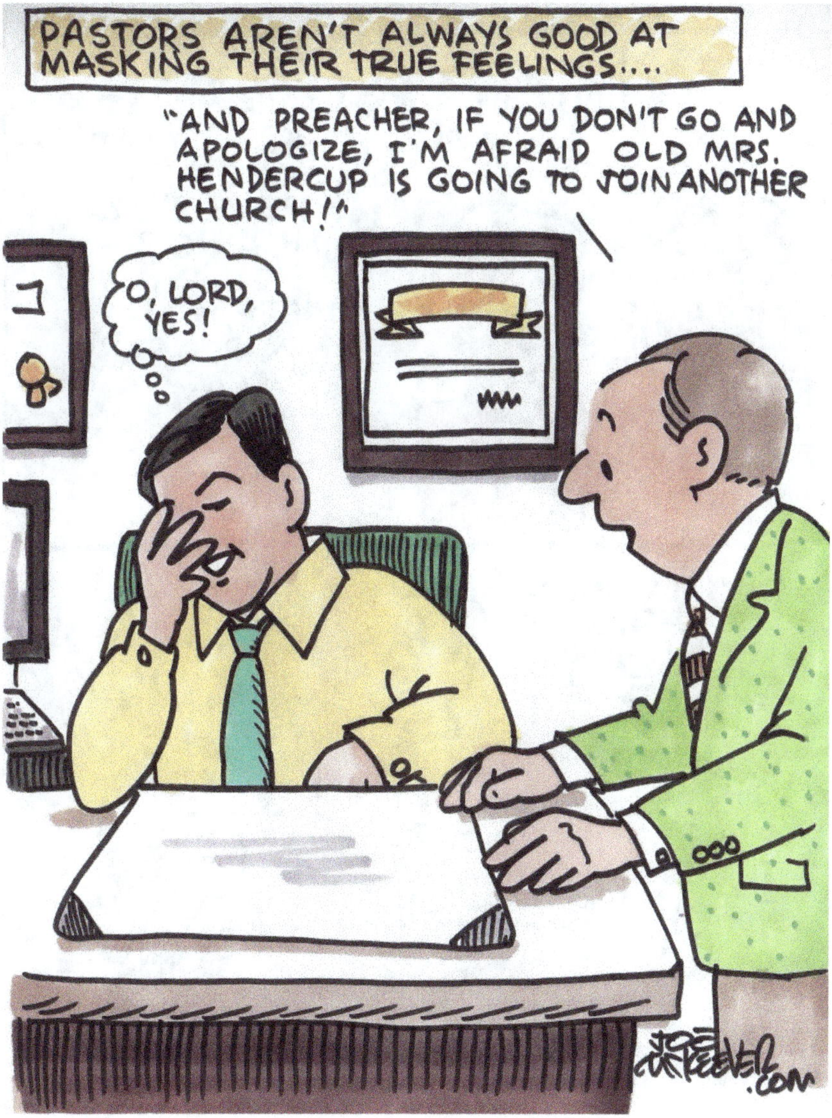
PASTORS AREN'T ALWAYS GOOD AT MASKING THEIR TRUE FEELINGS....
"AND PREACHER, IF YOU DON'T GO AND APOLOGIZE, I'M AFRAID OLD MRS. HENDERCUP IS GOING TO JOIN ANOTHER CHURCH!"
O, LORD, YES!
.COM

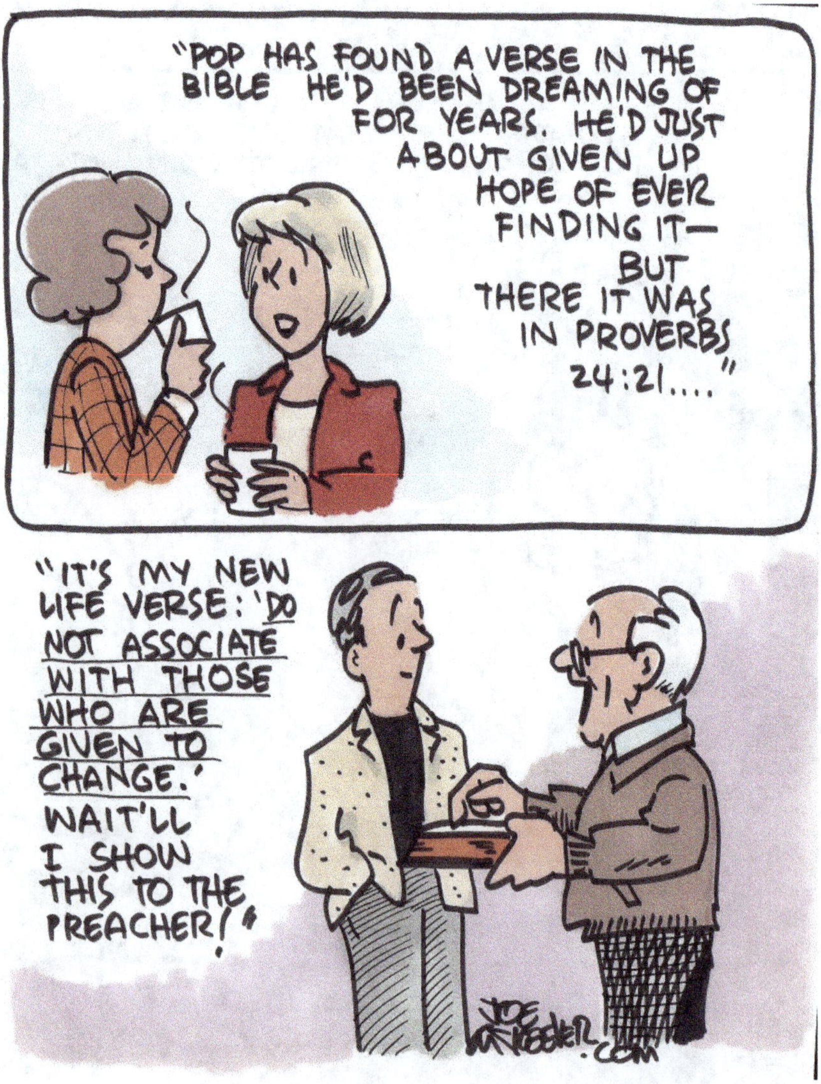
"POP HAS FOUND A VERSE IN THE BIBLE HE'D BEEN DREAMING OF FOR YEARS. HE'D JUST ABOUT GIVEN UP HOPE OF EVER FINDING IT— BUT THERE IT WAS IN PROVERBS 24:21...."
"IT'S MY NEW LIFE VERSE: 'DO NOT ASSOCIATE WITH THOSE WHO ARE GIVEN TO CHANGE.' WAIT'LL I SHOW THIS TO THE PREACHER!"
JOE MCKEEVER.COM

"MY DEACONS ARE GETTING SUSPICIOUS OF OUR WEEKLY SESSIONS—THEY THINK I'M SEEING ANOTHER CHURCH ON THE SIDE."

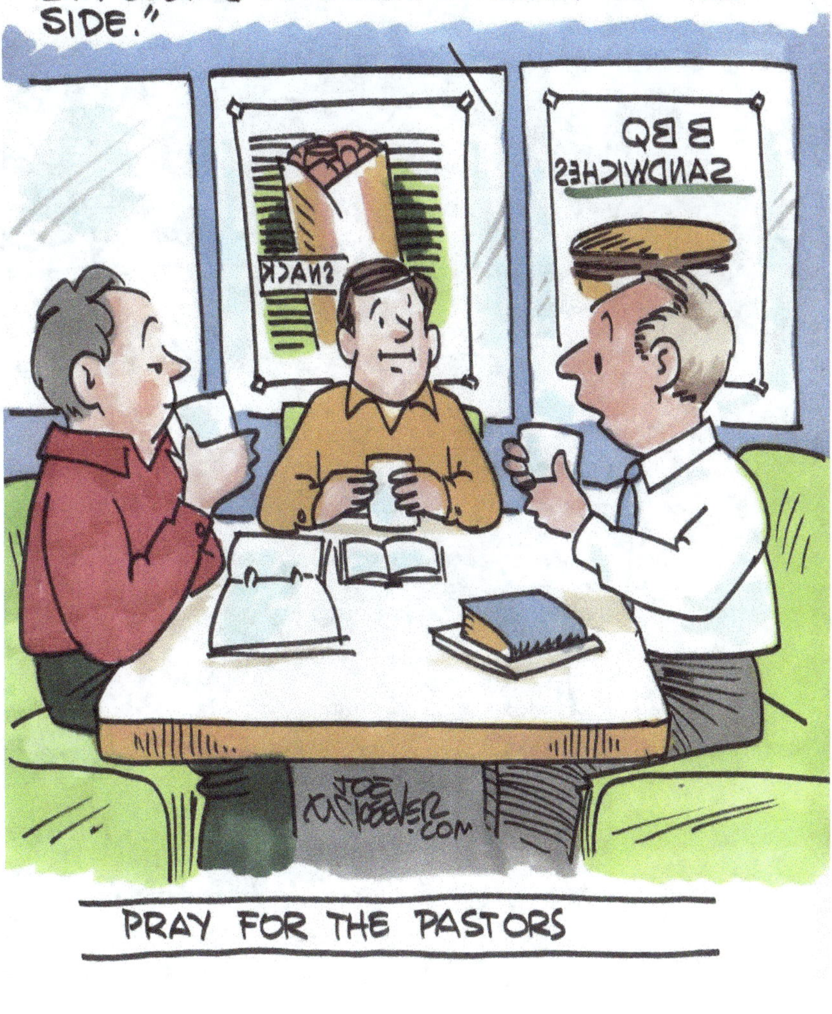
JOE McKEEVER.COM

PRAY FOR THE PASTORS

"THE PASTOR WILL NOT MISS ME WHILE WE'RE ON VACATION. I'VE ARRANGED FOR DEACON MOORE TO CRITIQUE HIS SERMONS IN MY ABSENCE."

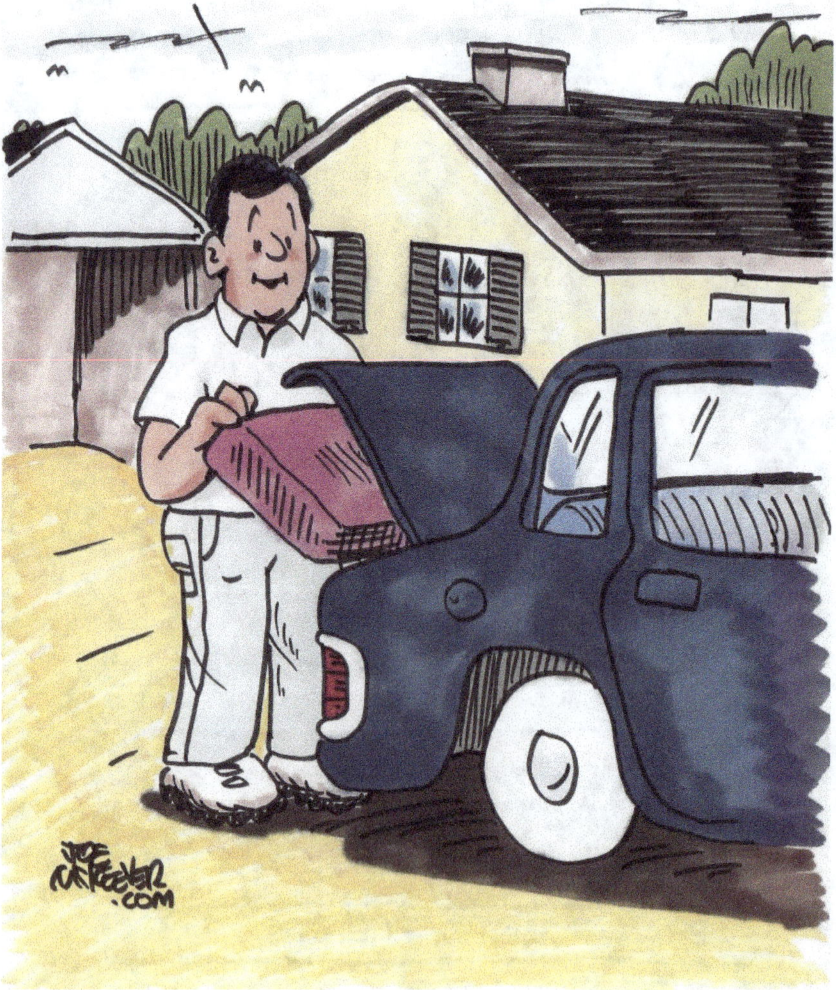
JOE MCKEEVER .COM

"WE'VE NEVER HAD AN ACTUAL PASTOR TO VISIT IN OUR HOME. YOU SEEM RATHER NORMAL."

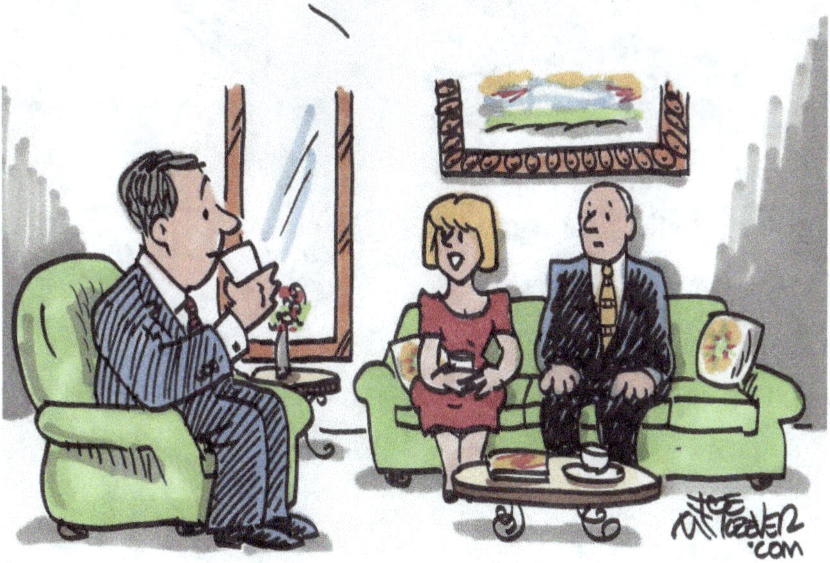

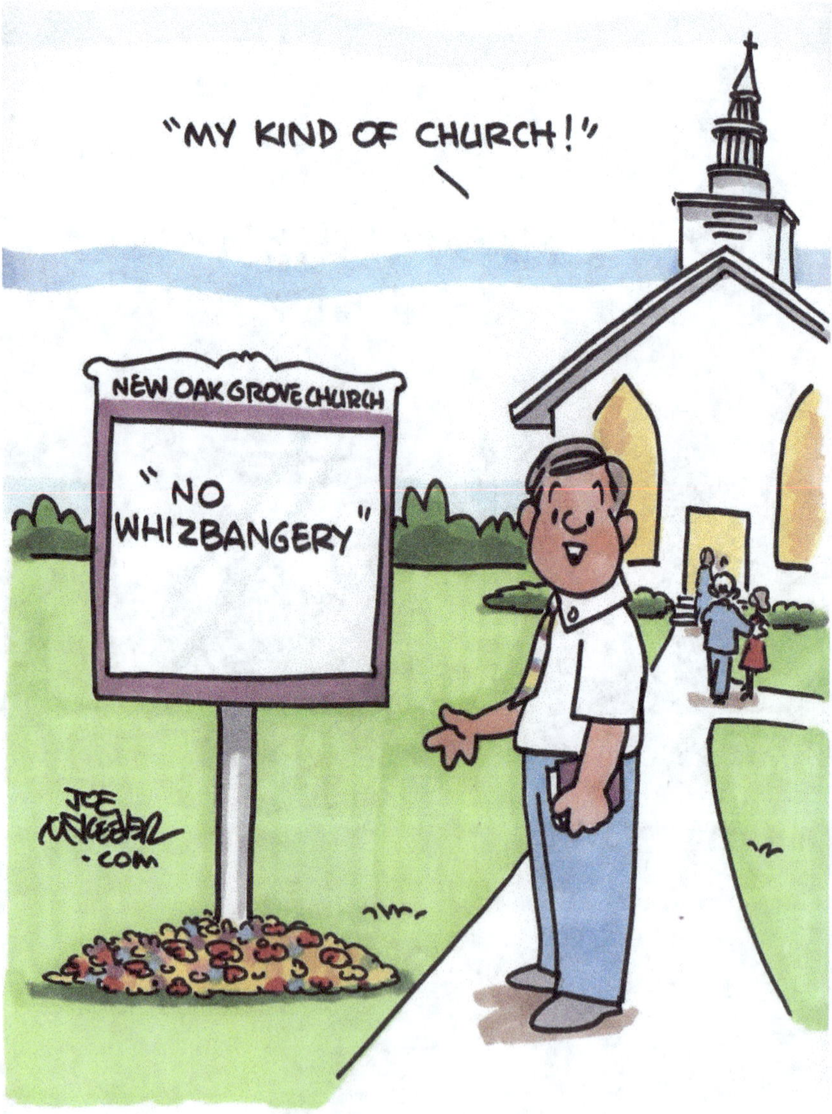
"MY KIND OF CHURCH!"
NEW OAK GROVE CHURCH
"NO WHIZBANGERY"
JOE MCKEEVER .com

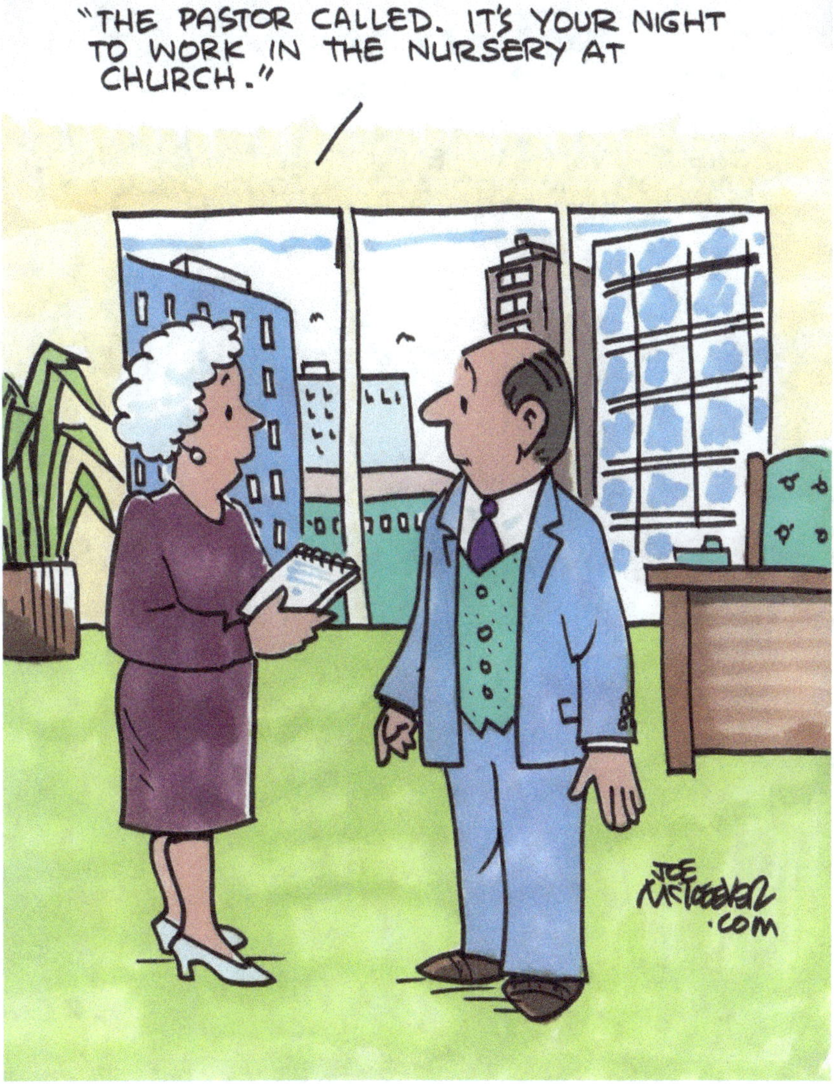
"THE PASTOR CALLED. IT'S YOUR NIGHT TO WORK IN THE NURSERY AT CHURCH."
JOE McKEEVER .COM

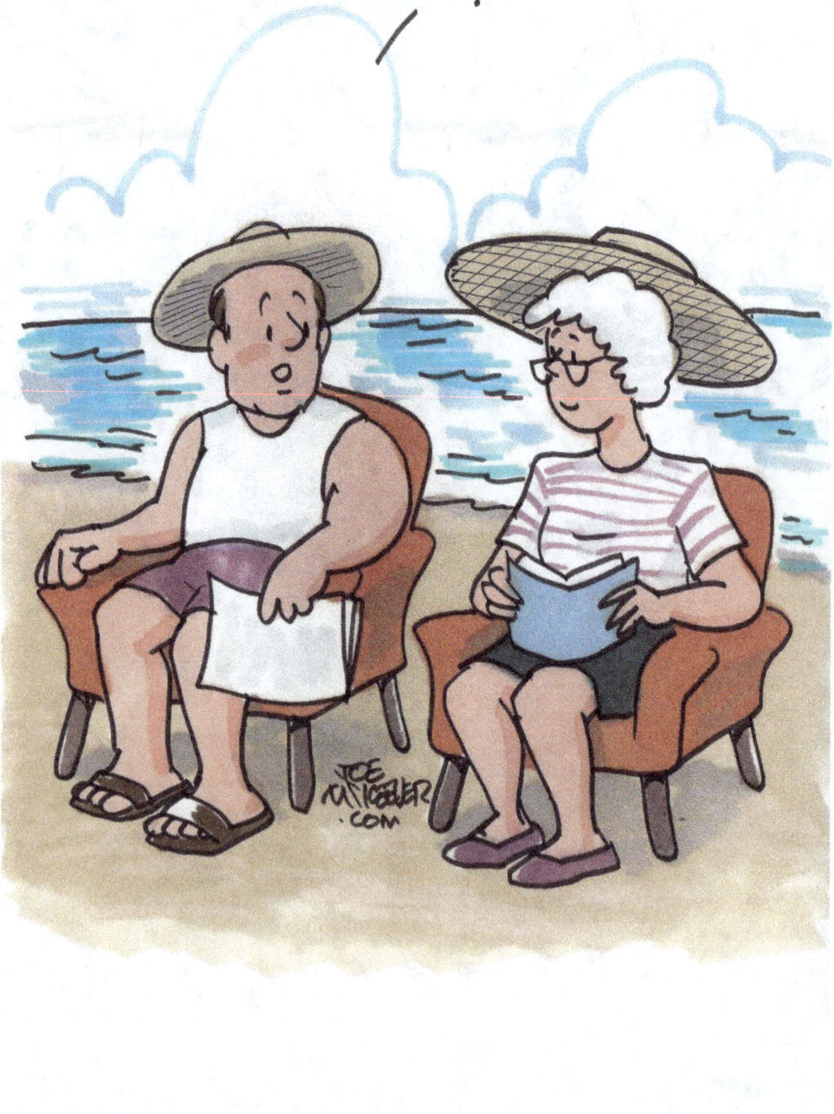

"I JUST HAVE THIS FEELING THAT THEY'LL CANCEL CHURCH IF I'M NOT AT THE SOUTH DOOR HANDING OUT BULLETINS!"

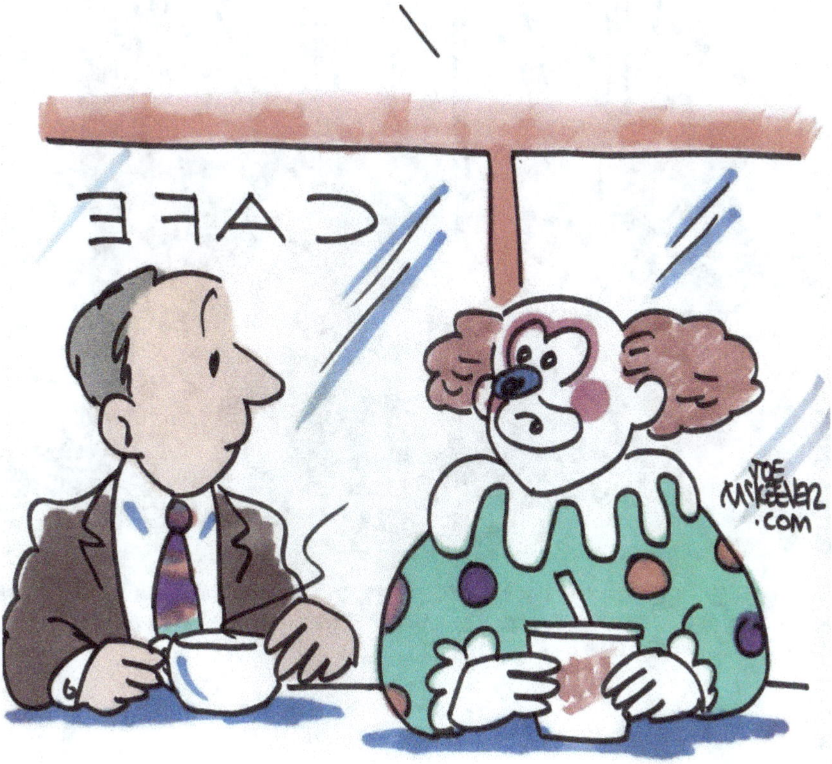
JOE MCKEEVER.COM

"THERE'S SOMETHING FUNNY ABOUT YOUR NEW PREACHER."

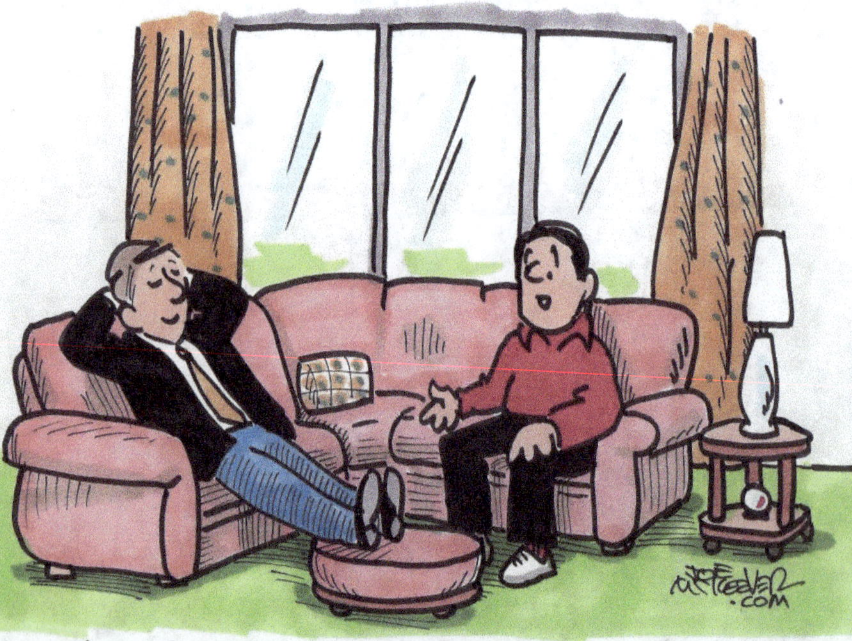

"THERE! I FEEL SO MUCH BETTER NOW. THANK YOU FOR TAKING TIME OUT OF YOUR BUSY DAY TO LISTEN TO MY TROUBLES, PASTOR. UH, PASTOR...."

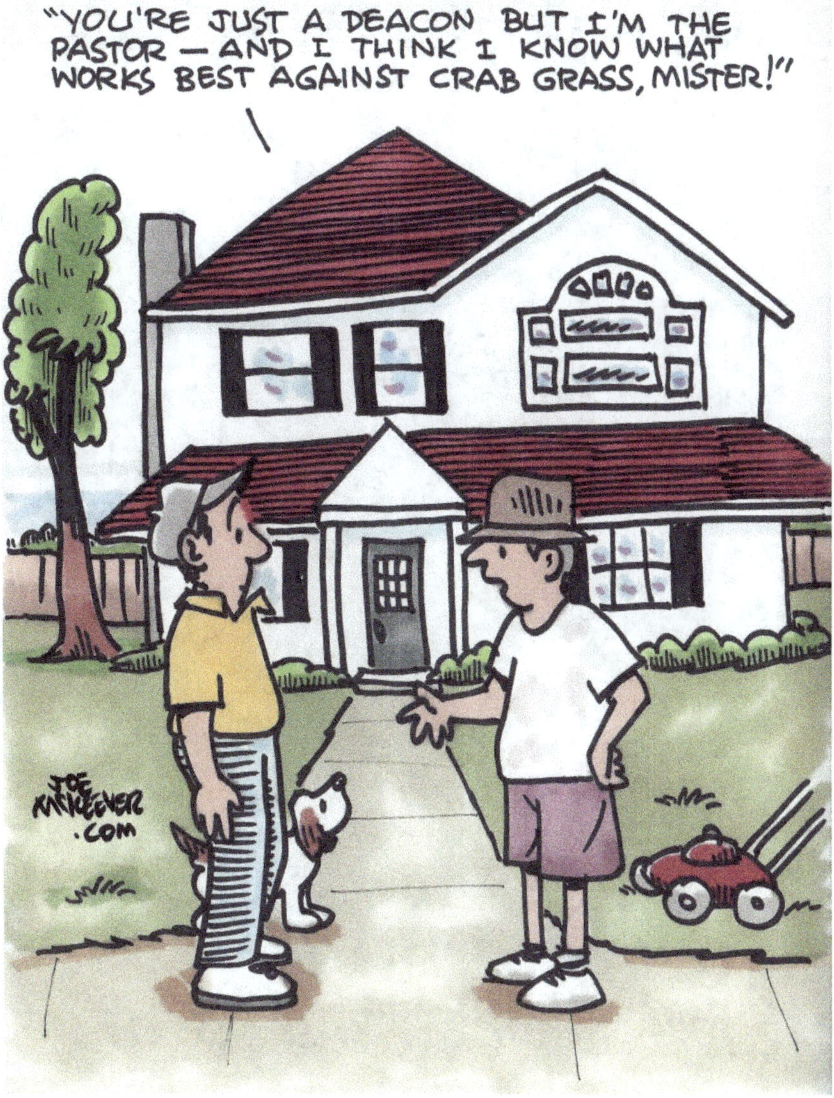
"YOU'RE JUST A DEACON BUT I'M THE PASTOR — AND I THINK I KNOW WHAT WORKS BEST AGAINST CRAB GRASS, MISTER!"
JOE McKEEVER .com

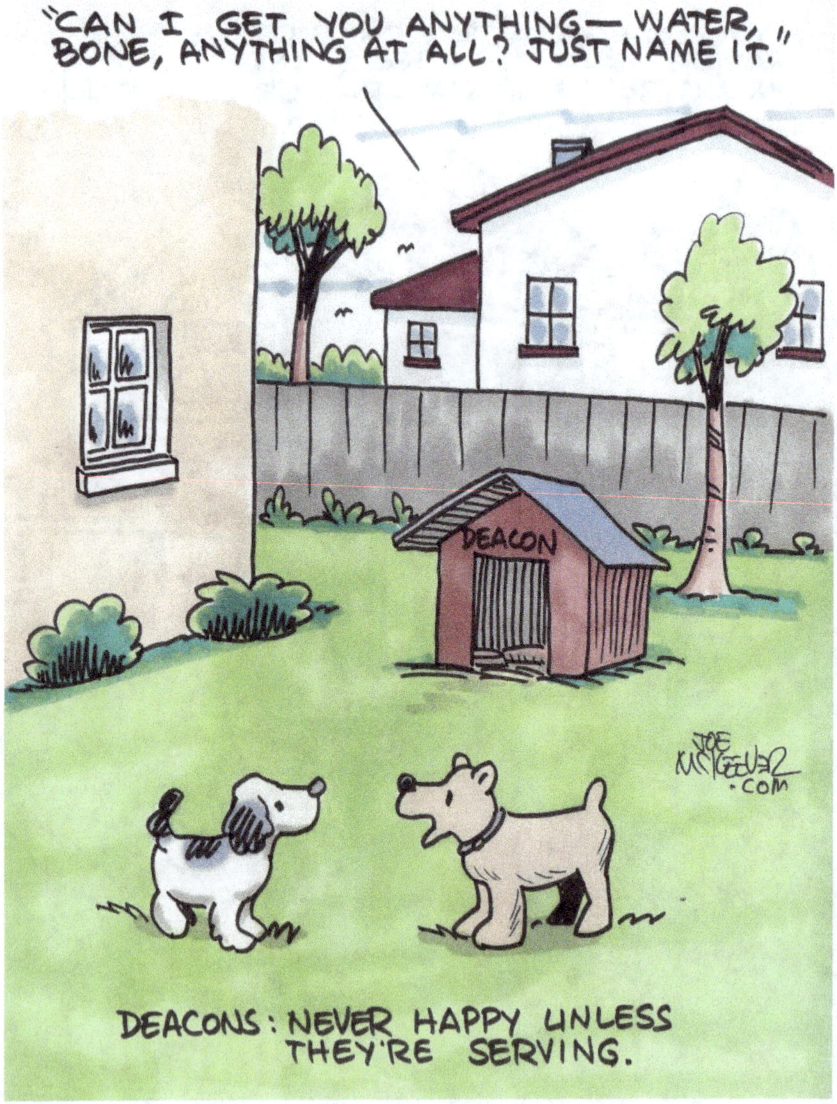
"CAN I GET YOU ANYTHING— WATER, BONE, ANYTHING AT ALL? JUST NAME IT."
DEACON
JOE MCGEEVER .COM
DEACONS: NEVER HAPPY UNLESS THEY'RE SERVING.

IMMEDIATELY FOLLOWING THE DEACONS MEETING, PASTOR BOB MODERATED A CHURCH BUSINESS SESSION, THEN RUSHED TO THE CEMETERY FOR A FUNERAL OF A DEAR FRIEND. AN HOUR LATER, HE HELD TWO COUNSELING SESSIONS, AND THAT NIGHT, PERFORMED A WEDDING. BOB IS A TYPICAL PASTOR.

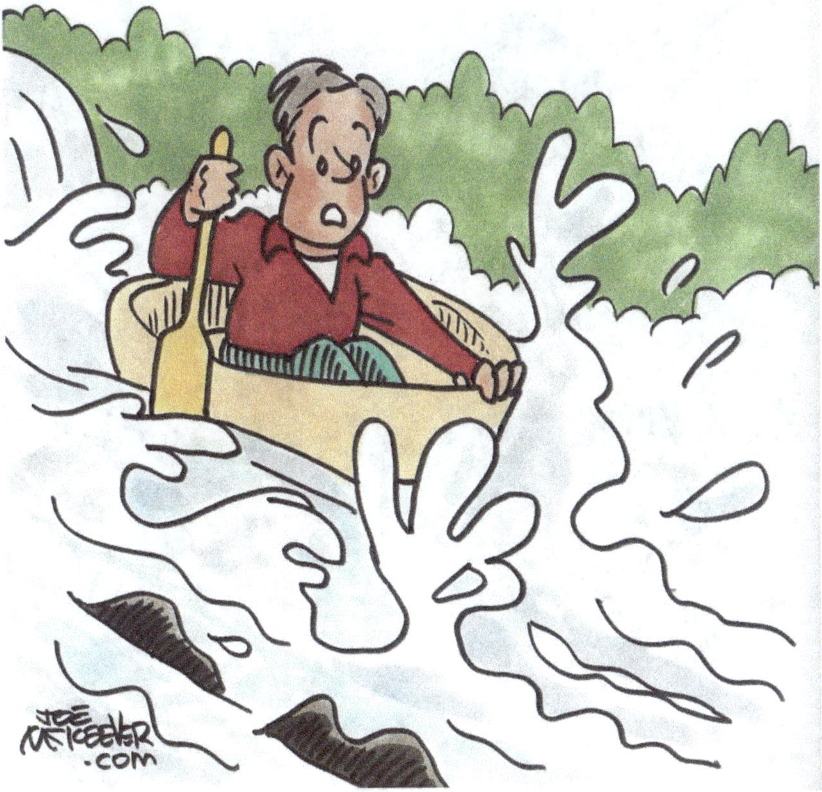
JOE MCKEEVER
.com

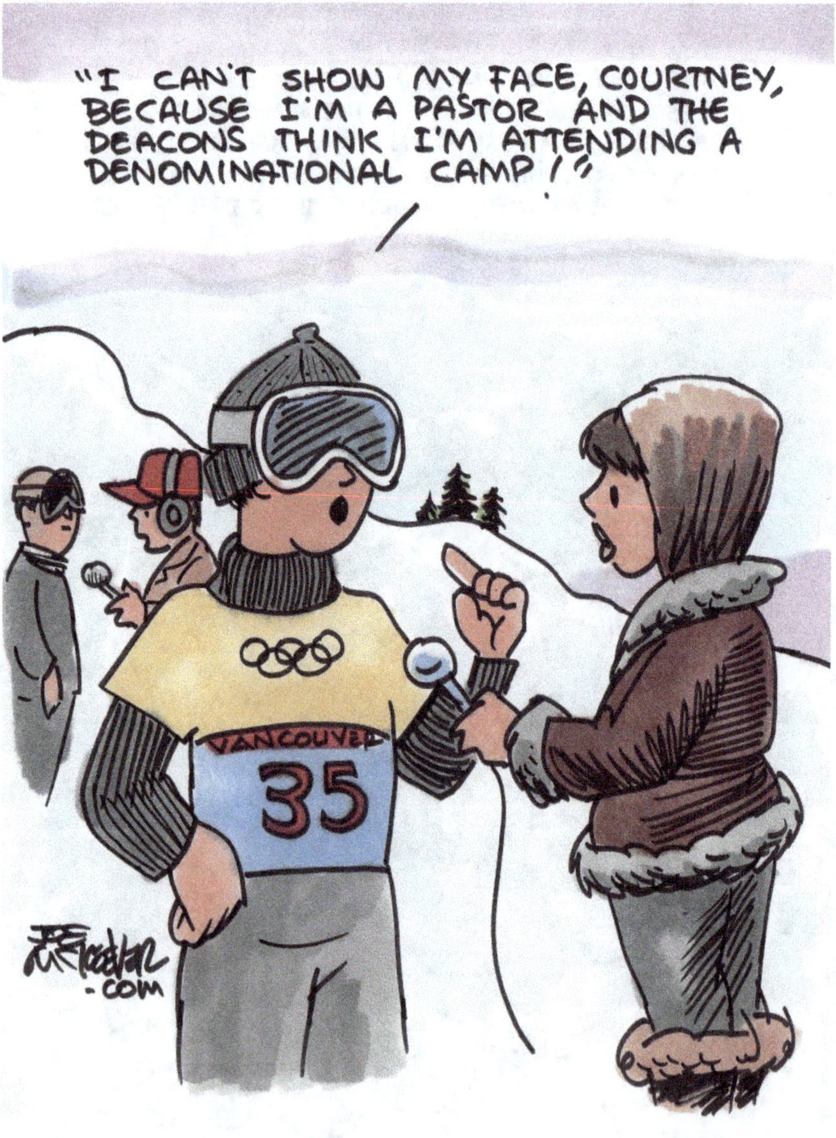
VANCOUVER
35
JOE MCKEEVER.COM

"I CAN'T SHOW MY FACE, COURTNEY, BECAUSE I'M A PASTOR AND THE DEACONS THINK I'M ATTENDING A DENOMINATIONAL CAMP!"

VALENTINE CARDS
from the PASTOR to the DEACONS
TO MY FAVORITE DEACON—
THANK YOU!
BLESS YOU!
Your pastor treasures you—
THE OTHER PREACHERS THINK ME A FREAK— OF ALL MY BUDDIES I LOVE MY DEKE!
I COUNT ON YOU TO SAVE MY HIDE; YOU COUNT ON ME— IT'S QUITE A RIDE!
OF ALL THE OCEANS IN ALL THE WORLD, IN ALL THE OYSTERS, YOU ARE THE PEARL!

www.ingramcontent.com/pod-product-compliance
Lightning Source LLC
Chambersburg PA
CBHW072114290426
44110CB00014B/1908